JOURNEYS OF A SUFI MUSICIAN

Kudsi Erguner

Journeys of a Sufi Musician

Translated from the French by
Annette Courtenay Mayers

SAQI

With thanks for all the help of Carole Fish, Adelaide Franca, Wendy Harries, Treffy Heard, Julian Keable, Adam Nott, Ben Pearce-Higgins and Caroline Reed.

British Library Cataloguing-in-Publication Data
A catalogue record for this book is available from the British Library

ISBN 0-86356-547-6
EAN 9-780863-565472

Published in French as *La fontaine de la séparation*
by Le bois d'Orion, L'Isle-sur-la-Sorgue, 2005

This edition first published 2005

SAQI
26 Westbourne Grove
London W2 5RH
www.saqibooks.com

A man, falling into a well, just manages to hang on to a dead branch of a tree growing around it. The branch nearly splits. A fatal fall is imminent. He then notices, with fright, that a dragon at the bottom of the well is trying to get hold of his legs. Mastering his fear, he sees, close to him, a beehive full of honey. While holding on with one hand, he takes a little honey with the other, tastes it and says, 'Life, what a joy!'

Fariduddin Attâr

I dedicate this book to my wife Arzu, and to my children Selman, Sinan and Merve: the honey of my life.

Contents

Foreword

Kudsi Erguner was born into the chaos of traditions lost, traditions destroyed, into a Turkey half East and half West, struggling to be modern, Western and secular, proud of, yet resenting its Ottoman past, militaristic and democratic, failing to stamp out a nostalgia for religion whilst jealously preserving a secret knowledge.

Kudsi's tale is the story of our time, of a searcher guided by a living tradition. Sufism knows no intermediaries. It has no dogmas; it is an opening towards the timeless, to the ever-present. Kudsi was especially fortunate through his family to grow up with Sufi music, to be linked to pure sound, to a sacred instrument, the *ney*, whose life is a direct expression of the quality of the one who breathes. Kudsi is restless, he travels with excitement, he sees the decay, the eroding of values but discovers how what is lost can be found again.

Twice his adventures brought us together and as we worked, I discovered a very special companion, a sensitive artist and, to this day, a warm friend.

In the mystery we call life, there is one painful conundrum. How can religion be a source of true understanding and at the same moment the source of such endless and cruel misunderstandings? If we follow Kudsi through these chapters, we live this question with him in his thoughts, his interrogations and in the practical details of his daily life.

Peter Brook, 2004

Introduction

The study of history has always seemed to me like a lesson in morality, which shows the ephemeral character of man, of civilisations, empires, traditions … and this in spite of their wish to be everlasting.

During my short life to date, I have witnessed the disappearance of many trees, which over centuries have offered men their shade and their fruit.

Through the story of my life, I want to reocunt the last moments of the Sufi tradition in Turkey. This tradition has been a light towards a true life and a great source of inspiration for the arts, an example of the art of living in harmony and a lesson in humanity.

I want, without controversy, to expose the neglect and demise of the values of this tradition, at a time when they could be of use as never before. I know I could be accused of being nostalgic about old times, or of taking refuge in a tradition in order to escape the realities of our time. But Sufism, as taught to me, is a way that shows how to live in the present, unencumbered by traditional forms while still being nourished by the deep meaning of sacred teachings and the exemplary lives of the prophets and Sufi masters. I am trying to be a man of faith who seeks to deepen religious meaning: to be a traditionalist without being dogmatic like one who does not appreciate the living nature of what is transmitted. The value of a diamond does not depend on whether it is old or new, but to the fact that it is a diamond. In the past, people sometimes mistook simple stones for jewels, and nowadays might throw away diamonds on the pretext that they are 'outdated'.

When I settled in France, I observed that paradoxically there were more Europeans capable of appreciating the values of my culture than people in my own country. I was able to confirm for myself and for my countrymen that Sufism and the arts inspired by it are not so much the concern of a nation or a particular cultural domain, but constitute a universal heritage whose values are not limited by time or space.

Some of the events that I relate in this book concern the political life of Turkey. My country was the first Muslim state to take the path of modernisation and in so doing became an example for others. In Turkish one uses the word *siyaset* to refer to 'government'. This word means 'cart driver', for it is a question of creating harmony between the horses who pull the cart, so that all their strengths and motives are unified. In this sense, man also needs a government to manage his own life, because the forces that move him are many: he is like a cart pulled by thousands of horses.

I think it is important to note that, as in many Muslim countries, owing to the mistakes of its 'cart drivers', Turkey is in a state of chaos caused by a race between its fastest horses. This can affect the search for a government which would allow men to manage their own lives better.

Another theme developed in this book is the image Eastern people have of the West and which Westerners have of the East. It is normal to escape into imagination when the world in which one lives proves to be disappointing.

However, I noticed that very often this attitude nurtures false hope. For me, the East has no geographical border, but is the direction of the rising sun of hope. The West, therefore, is situated where night begins. Wherever a man may be, he is obliged to live both day and night, at the point where The Fountain of Separation (see Chapter Sixteen) rises and from where he can start a journey towards dawn.

I would like to thank Nezih Uzel, who has always encouraged me to write about what we have shared; and Jean-Michel Ricard who, with great patience and love, agreed to put in writing what I had told him.

God is *Settar*, that is to say, He puts a veil on the shames of our lives. If I appear in this text to be a pretentious man who purports to reveal what God has hidden from people, it is simply to evoke in my readers a certain prudence in their search for Truth; to suggest that they look for He whose virtues are reflected in the mirrors of human beings, and not human beings who appear to be virtuous.

Kudsi Erguner, 2004

ONE

The Hand of Myriam

As Celâleddin Rumi says in his *Mesnevî*, there are three apocalypses for human beings. The first is birth, the second, death and the third, resurrection of all in front of Truth. My first apocalypse took place, according to the Christian calendar, on the 4th of February 1952. By chance, I was born in a town in Eastern Turkey: Diyarbakir, where my mother's grandfather had an official function at the time.

My grandmother herself was born in that region. I was told that she belonged to an *ansari* family from Medina. Medina, in the Islamic world, is known for being the city in which the Prophet was welcomed after he had been thrown out by the unbelievers of his own city, Mecca.

I was born in a house architecturally typical of the region. The various rooms were situated around a patio, with an ornamental pool in the middle. There was no communication between the rooms. One had to go across the patio to pass from one room to another. This was the place of my first apocalypse. It wasn't a real one because, as my mother told me later, the delivery went very well. The custom, in this circumstance, is for someone to bring the bud of a lotus flower and place it in a vase next to the woman in labour. (In Turkish, the name of the lotus flower is translated as 'Mary's hand'.) At the same time a *zikr* begins, with the repetition of the phrase *La ilaha illa Allah Muhammad Rasul Allah*: 'There is no other God but Allah, Muhammad is His Prophet'. (In the *zikr* [Arabic: *dhikr*], or 'invocation', the name of God is intoned repeatedly.)

This ceremony of the *zikr* and my mother's cries of pain mingled at the heart of this ancient stone house in the town of Diyarbakir. Her gaze, fixed on the lotus bud, awaited its opening which, according to tradition, would happen at the time of birth. And so it was: just as the flower burst open, I was born.

Soon after, my mother took me to Ankara, where my father was working at the time. He came from a family which had lived in Istanbul for several generations. In the East there is no aristocracy, so we have little knowledge of our ancestors, and the genealogy of our families is very incomplete. I can, however, go back with certainty to my great-grandfather, who was the *imam* and *türbedar* (an honorific title given to a guardian) of the Mausoleum of Sultan Yavuz Selim. This mausoleum is in Istanbul on one of the hills at the edge of the Golden Horn.

We left Ankara in 1953, after the death of my paternal grandfather. My father wished to work in the city of Istanbul. The house in which my great-grandfather and my grandfather lived was very near the mosque where the mausoleum of Yavuz Selim is situated. This quarter, which today is still called by the name of this *sultan*, was at that time much prized because many of the wooden houses perched up on this hill had a splendid view of the Golden Horn and of Istanbul. A little further on is the hill where the café frequented by the French novelist and celebrated traveller Pierre Loti can be found.

Unfortunately, Istanbul was often prey to fires, and many of the inhabitants lost all their belongings. One spark was enough to set these old wooden houses on fire, and gradually the flames could ravage entire districts – so much so that the inhabitants ended up accepting with fatalism the tragic destiny of being left without shelter. Fire mixed closely with the everyday life of Istanbul inhabitants.

A great Sufi master, Ibrahim Kuşadali (1774–1845), who owned a wooden tekke [gathering-place] surrounded by several wooden houses, was with his disciples one day. The conversation, quite subtle and moving, was suddenly interrupted by a disciple who announced the outbreak of fire in a nearby district. The master, a little upset by this interruption, nevertheless went on speaking. Soon after, the same disciple, even more worried, entered the room: 'Master, master, this time it is our own district which is starting to burn.' Taking no notice, the master continued his discourse. The next time, the disciple announced that now the fire was in their street, but he wasn't listened to any more than before. At last, the disciple, panic-stricken, came back to announce that the flames were licking the tekke itself. So the master got up, and said, simply, 'Let's continue elsewhere.'

That was the way the inhabitants of Istanbul reacted: they were going to continue their lives elsewhere. Little by little the wooden houses were replaced by stone, mostly constructed in Western styles. My family also had a house built in stone in another quarter of Istanbul, on land which was bought by incurring a number of debts. We moved into this new house, sharing it, as was the custom at that time, with my grandmother, my aunt, my uncle – in short, my father's family.

The fires punctuated my childhood. My friends and I were hypnotised by the gigantic flames. Later I became interested in the philosophical meaning of fires when mentioned in folktales. In particular, I was amazed by a Buddhist parable which corresponded very well with the situation in Istanbul:

On returning home, a man found his house in flames. In a panic, knowing that his two children were inside, absorbed in their games, and that they would not realise the danger, the father called out, shouting to warn them – but without success as they were lost in their play. Then, tricking them, he called, 'Come, come, I've brought you some toys!' This time the children heard and rushed towards their father. Buddha concluded: 'This world is on fire. You are called to be saved, but you are distracted by a game. To be convinced, you have to be offered toys.'

One of the first memories I have of the Istanbul of my childhood, unlike the concrete-covered Istanbul of today, is that of a town full of gardens, parks, vegetable plots and empty spaces that surrounded the *mahalle* (district). The inhabitants lived close to each other, forming well-bonded communities. The dogs, and even the cats, formed an integral part of the district. Free to go where they liked, they were fed by everyone and, in exchange, as well as offering their affection, they mounted guard at night. As a result, it was impossible for a stranger to walk in these streets without being followed by a pack of dogs, each one barking louder than the other. In the evening, it was very frightening to go through another district guarded by watchdogs who didn't know us.

We spent a happy childhood, playing under the trees, gathering figs, nuts, apples and pears. It was a country life right in the midst of the Istanbul that has nowadays become a great metropolis of more than 15 million inhabitants. At that time there were no wide boulevards. Private cars were still rare, and the streets were used almost exclusively by the tramways which assured public transport.

Winter and summer, the streets were busy with children's games. Football came to be our favourite distraction, although it was not as popular as it has become today. Instead of a football we had to use a ball made of tightly crumpled newspaper tied with string. Real footballs were far too expensive for our parents' modest budget. Nevertheless, to be able to get one, I decided with a friend that we had to find the necessary money by ourselves. This is when the idea came to us to make and sell lemonade. At the other end of our district, there was a small area where adolescents and adults came to play football from time to time. We decided to install our business there. We each pinched a few lemons from the family kitchen, and one of us borrowed a bucket and some glasses which we filled with the lemonade we made. At the end of the match, from the edge of the football pitch, we shouted: 'Who wants lemonade?' In less time than it takes to tell, our bucket was empty. But when we asked to be paid, all we got was a few kicks on the bottom. We went home in despair, with tears in our eyes. To crown it all, we each received a good spanking by our parents for having stolen the lemons. This first business failure of ours was not enough to discourage us. Some time later, another idea came to us to make *ayran* (a refreshing drink made of yogurt diluted with water) and sell it in the streets. We set off along the streets with our bucket of *ayran*. We had agreed that neither of us should touch the drink, but the heat at that time of the year was such that my friend offered me the one and only coin he had to have the right to drink a glass of it. It took hardly any time for me to be tortured by thirst. So I gave him back his coin in exchange for the right to drink a glass myself. From street to street, and thirst to thirst, the coin changed hands between him and me until the bucket was half-empty. If we succeeded in selling several glasses of *ayran* the money we received that day was far from sufficient to buy a football. These two small 'business ventures' nipped in the bud any vague desire to go into business in the future.

The streets were full of peddlers, which we had tried in vain to imitate. Many, with diverse and varied cries, called out to both adults and children. The one we liked most was the *macun* (marshmallow) salesman. He offered beautiful colourful sweets, displayed on a large metal tray. For a few pence, we could get a little stick on which there was a small lump of this wonderful mouth-watering sweet.

Often, these peddlers were accompanied by a clarinet player and a *darbouka* (percussion instrument) player. The musicians attracted the adults to the windows, and the children then cried out to their parents to throw them a few pence to buy some marshmallow: a rather clever sales trick!

Another favourite of the children was the bear trainer. He would turn the corner of the street with his bear at the end of a chain and play enthusiastically on his tambourine to signal their arrival. The children gathered around him, but they weren't the audience he wanted. What he was looking for was the money from the shopkeepers or from the housewives, who never failed to come to their windows. The show began with a bear dance. Then the bear trainer would make the audience laugh, especially the women, by telling the story of the young bride who fainted when she saw her mother-in-law in the *hammam* (Turkish bath). The story was mimed by the bear who lay on the ground and pretended to faint. This was a guaranteed success with the women in the audience. Sometimes the bear leader would challenge the men and invite anyone courageous enough to confront the bear with his bare hands. Anyone who could turn the bear over onto his back would win a certain amount of money. For us children, these matches between our local grocer or carpenter and the bear were always very surprising, not to say impressive. When no one took up the challenge, the bear trainer himself would fight with his own beast.

All the children were a long way from having the few pence needed to satisfy their appetites. At every stall that interested the forty-odd kids who were there in the street, one could hear a unanimous chorus of young voices asking for pennies from their mothers.

There was at that time a very popular singer in Istanbul called Zeki Müren. He was a transvestite endowed with a very beautiful voice. He was much appreciated by women, not only because of the fine quality of his voice, but also because he had introduced 'Hollywood' fashions into Turkey.

There were many street singers who sang the latest hits, imitating his voice. Amongst them was a boy who was a bit simple, but who had a very fine voice. The young girls of the neighbourhood were mad about him, partly because of the quality of his voice and also because of his fine physique. When he sang, the girls made a circle around him. We never missed a chance to tease him. His singing was not nearly as intriguing as the spicy repartee he exchanged with the girls. These innocent, playful matches always ended with bursts of laughter. We often interrupted our games so as not to miss any part of this amusing spectacle.

In the summer holidays, a happy custom demanded that the children work with an artisan. So the hairdresser, the grocer and the carpenter would employ us to do small jobs. The most sought-after jobs were with the carpenter, as we could pretend to be working while we were actually making toys out of leftover bits of wood. I had the privilege of ending up with our neighbour, a carpenter. In his workshop, I made a scooter out of a plank with two castors and a handlebar. With this contraption, I used to go to the end of the street to reach the one and only sloping asphalt boulevard. Down I would go, not without risk, making a hell of a racket.

During this season, as the habit of going away on holiday did not yet exist and the weather was very hot, grown-ups also went out into the street. In the evening, one or another of the neighbours would spread a carpet on the ground and invite the women to drink tea. As for the men, they gathered around another tray of tea a little further away. It was a good excuse for the children to play later than usual.

This family-like life amongst neighbours demanded a particular code of behaviour based on mutual respect. Privacy was practically non-existent. Children knew all about the arguments between husbands and wives. Everybody knew everything about everybody, but all were expected to respect the dignity of others. Socially speaking the inhabitants were mostly artisans, small shopkeepers or civil servants, who were very numerous in Turkey at that time. All had more or less the same income.

Amongst the civil servants in that district was a customs officer, who one day came home driving a car which he parked outside his front door. This caused a great deal of gossip amongst his neighbours. Everywhere one could hear: 'How did he manage to buy himself a car!?' To justify himself he pretended that a friend had given it to him. It was strongly suspected that a bribe had been taken, and he and his family were seen in a bad light by the whole street. Finally they felt obliged to move house. Living near a thief or a man suspected of living by dishonest means was regarded as a strain upon the whole neighbourhood. Nowadays one might think that such strong bonds uniting neighbouring families would be rather heavy to bear, but at the time it did not seem so to us.

In the early Sixties, Istanbul was experiencing the first waves of immigration from the provinces. Flats were built to meet the need for cheap accommodation. One saw many four- or five-storey blocks of flats all built more or less in the same style. Today one can still see these hideous buildings covered with the multicoloured mosaics which were in fashion at that time. The building sites provided all sorts of materials which we children would retrieve and make things to play with. The little pieces of mosaic found in the builders' rubble were seen as precious treasures, and served as currency for making bets or exchanging goods. These were happy days when all we had to play with was what the street was kind enough to give us. Great joy could spring from the most worthless piece of rubbish.

As ready-to-wear clothes did not yet exist, there was a great diversity of clothing. In winter, we wore knitted pullovers and trousers made by our mothers. Women had to make their children's clothes as well as doing all the housework. One rarely passed a house without hearing the hum of a sewing machine. Singer sewing machines were in vogue; a very popular song of the day extolled their merits.

Anything to do with food was obviously a woman's business. One had to preserve certain foods to be able to use them out of season. Tomatoes, gherkins and all sorts of vegetables were pickled in vinegar. Usually, at the end of the season, a day was appointed for the women to gather together and help each other with the preparation of these pickles.

During the months of the year when the fruit and vegetables were in season, they could be bought from the greengrocers who pushed their barrows from street to street, filling the air with the smell of tomatoes, cherries, melons and watermelons. Having to wait for a particular fruit or vegetable to be in season increased tenfold the pleasure we had in eating them. Furthermore, if the produce (watermelons, for example) was sufficiently heavy to need a horse and cart, the children were allowed to pat the horse, and even to get up onto the cart. To this day, when I see a watermelon, I cannot stop from associating its scent with the smell of horse.

All these barrow boys had their own methods of attracting custom. At that time, plastic was new, and it was all the rage. The trick used by one peddler for getting rid of his merchandise was to exchange new plastic plates for copperware in every household. To demonstrate the merits of plastic, he had a way of throwing a plate high into the sky. When it returned intact, the housewives, amazed, were unable to resist the virtues of this revolutionary dish, which was not only unbreakable but, unlike copper, would not need re-tinning. So every woman ran to her house to bring out all her copper dishes to exchange them for these miraculous plastic ones. This is how magnificent vessels used for generations, as well as rugs and *kilims* (which the merchants were also far from disdaining as means of exchange) disappeared from many homes.

All the coming and going of itinerant vendors did not stop mothers from going regularly on Fridays to market. It was a huge place, and full of life. Children often went with their mothers to help carry back the shopping. There was a very particular code of conduct which everyone had to respect. So as not to encourage covetousness, neighbours had to ignore what others brought back from the market. If, for example, a woman saw some aubergines in a neighbour's basket when they were exorbitantly priced, and if she herself didn't have the means to buy them, what could she say to her children when they asked her for some? If she caught sight of the aubergines, the neighbour would have been obliged to offer her some, or to bring her some of the dish that she made with them. This custom was called 'the right to see'. When the net shopping bag was first introduced (incidentally, it was called 'the French shopping bag'), replacing the closed-basket *zenbil,* it caused an uproar. Some housewives thought this shopping bag was more European, and therefore more chic. Their neighbours would say behind their back, 'Did you see, she's using a French shopping bag! Really, she's going too far!' This respect for one's neighbour also held true when strong cooking smells came from the kitchen. Then it was necessary to have the foresight to prepare an extra amount of food for the children to take to the neighbours. It was one way of apologising, and allowing them to taste the dish that was the origin of the provocative smell.

This type of community life brought a rhythm to the activities of the house. A certain day was reserved for the laundry, another for beating the carpets, etc. That is to say, in every household the same tasks were performed on the same day. This arrangement allowed the women to share their free time.

One day a *bekçi,* a kind of district supervisor or community policeman, came to announce to the inhabitants of our street that they would have to leave their homes on a particular day. As any child who is curious by nature, I asked my parents what it was about. They explained that the mosque that was just in front of our house was to be demolished because it was in the way of a new road with which the government had planned to link the airport to the centre of town. We had to leave our street in the hands of the *bekçi* and take temporary refuge with some neighbours who lived a few streets away, so that the mosque could be blown up.

The next day, when we returned, the minaret and the mosque were no longer there. It was very sad. A beautiful image from my childhood had been erased, replaced by a gigantic work site and the smell of asphalt which persisted for months. Once the road was finished, my friends and I spent whole days in the ablution pool of the no-longer-existing mosque. It was a huge marble fountain that could not be moved, Lord knows why! Perched up there, we amused ourselves counting cars, some watching one way and others in another direction. The winners were those who counted the most cars passing on their side; we reached five or six cars a day! Long gone was the time when we went to gather fruit ...

TWO

Amongst the Musicians and Dervishes of Istanbul

In Istanbul, until very recently, the life of traditional classical music was confined to private houses where, each week, the masters of music hosted their friends, pupils and a few music lovers. This is how on Tuesdays, my grandfather Suleyman Erguner, a musician of repute – at the same time composer and *ney* player – was host at his home in the Yavuz Selim district. My father, as the eldest son, in his turn took over this ancient tradition. Every Tuesday the house filled up with musicians: singers, *ud* players, *kemence* players and players of the *tanbur*.

These gatherings were very friendly, and in no way didactic or academic. Towards the end of the afternoon some venerable gentlemen would appear. I later learned that they were musicians of great repute. In the evening dinner was served, after which the musical event began. Great singers and instrumentalists could then be heard not only by the members of our community, but also by many of the inhabitants of the district. Those who were not fortunate enough to enter the little music room remained in the street – even in winter, despite the cold. Amongst these great musicians, there were singers such as Mecid Gürses and Esat Geredeli. The latter loved *ghazal*, and his voice was at the same time so sublime and so powerful that it could be heard far beyond our street. There was also Allaeddin Yavasça (who is still alive today), a great master of classical singing who was a pupil of my grandfather. Amongst the instrumentalists, there were many young men who have themselves become great masters.

For me, as a child, these gatherings were a great joy not only because of the music, which I was not yet able to appreciate for its true value (but which remained anchored forever in my memory), but also because everyone showed such kindness and exceptional tenderness towards us children. Far from being excluded from this world of adults, we were completely integrated and given even more consideration than any of us could have expected. This is why we waited impatiently for Tuesdays. After the death of my father these meetings took place at the house of Cahid Gozkan, an *ud* player who had also been my father's pupil. He owned a huge house in the very charming old quarter of Koca Mustafa Pasa, which commanded a view of the entrance to the Bosphorus. When he had to move, the meetings were held at his new place at Göztepe, at that time a little village in the Anatolian part of Istanbul.

Apart from these purely musical meetings, the dervish *tekke* were places where traditional musical knowledge and true Sufi music found their home. The same had happened in the past, when two schools existed side by side, one coming from the Ottoman court and the other from the Sufis. Although the Ottoman court eventually lost interest in traditional music in favour of European music, the *tekke* continued to be the home of great musicians until the present day.

In 1925, a law passed by the government of the completely new Turkish Republic prohibited Sufism (*tariqa*) and all the places where it was practised were forbidden. My father, like his ancestors before him, belonged to this community. As they all did, he played the *ney* at their ceremonies. This true micro-society, which was marginalised in Istanbul, lived in strict secrecy. By law, purely musical events were allowed, but meetings which had a ceremonial or religious aspect (*sama*) were strictly forbidden. Thus, it was indispensable for these communities to take certain precautions so as not to be disturbed.

One of these Sufi places was at Edirnekapi, on the edge of the Fatih district. It was built by the well-known architect Ekrem Hakki Ayverdi for his master Kenan Rufai, and was the last *tekke* to have been built. This wooden building included a vast ceremonial room. I remember that during the meetings, members of the brotherhood stood at each end of the street as lookouts to give warning of any police intervention. But I remember even better, although at that time I must have been hardly five or six years old, those old men with luminous faces, smiling and pleasant, whose eyes always appeared moist, as if they had just wiped away a tear at the sound of the *ney* or the recitation of a poem, or after the *zikr*.

Near our house was the *tekke* of Sümbül Sinan, who was the master of Suleyman the Magnificent (1520–66), the great Ottoman *sultan*. There, as a child, I attended several *sama'*. The last master of this *tekke* was called Nurullah Kiliç. One day, my father took me to this venerable old man to play the *ney*. On the way, he told me, 'You see, when I was your age, your grandfather took me to this *sheik* [master] just as I am doing with you now. This *sheik*, who has himself been a great player, owns a very rare collection. Maybe he will appreciate your playing and, being old, perhaps he will offer you one of his *ney*.' Even if that was not the only reason for our visit, at the back of our minds we had the secret hope of leavingwith one of these famous instruments. I played the *ney* for him and he patted my head, just as he had done with my father, assuring me that I would be a great *ney* player. But we left without one of the magnificent flutes, which we had had the time to glance at in a glass case during our visit ... We later learned that upon his death his children had sold his collection to tourists in the Great Bazaar.

As well as serving a ceremonial function, these meetings were also very convivial. The followers prepared food and drink for the several hundred people who attended. Apart from the *tekke* of Rufai, there was another in the Eyüp district, 'Eyüp' being the name of a Muslim saint who was killed in front of the walls of Constantinople. There were also several other *tekke* – notably that of Ummi Sinan, of which Nasuhi Bilmen was the last master . There, as in the meetings at Rufai's *tekke,* my father and his *ney* were looked forward to, just as his own father had been held in high esteem by the Sufi brotherhood of his time. Everyone who came to these gatherings was like part of my family. Their children were like my own brothers. It is important to note that there was no antagonism amongst the brotherhoods. Furthermore, the situation of prohibition was the same for all.

One of the places my parents frequented regularly was the Uzbek *tekke* in Usküdar. Usküdar was, at that time, a small village in the eastern part of Istanbul. Unlike the European district which was already beginning to be transformed, the Anatolian quarter remained much more traditional. At the top of a hill called Sultan Tepe ('The Sultan's Hill') there was a huge wooden building from which, beyond a grove, one could see the Bosphorus. Scattered over this hill were large *konak* (wooden houses), surrounded by vast and beautiful gardens.

For a time this *tekke*, which every Sunday welcomed a crowd of several hundred people, was privileged to escape some of the prohibitions which had hit the Sufi communities. The reason for this was that during the anti-colonial conflicts, which resulted in the creation of the Republic by Mustafa Kemal Atatürk, the independence movement had found refuge in this place. As the city of Istanbul was occupied by the British army, a number of independent intellectuals gathered in the Uzbek *tekke* before joining those who were in Anatolia.

Consequently, this *tekke* was considered a historic place inasmuch as it had supported the Republic in its early days. Almost the whole Sufi community of Istanbul was welcomed there, as well as a number of artists, musicians and poets. It was led by Sheik Necmeddin. In 1925, following the prohibitions which devastated Sufi activities in Turkey, the building and its contents were confiscated by the state.

Several *tekke* were converted into museums, such as the one at Pera in Istanbul dedicated to Galip Dede; others were transformed into mosques in which the former ceremonial room became the place of prayer. An *imam*, a civil servant from the Ministry of Religious Affairs, was in charge of these new mosques. Many of the *imams* had received their diplomas from the school of theology, which had been established by the government, and were suspicious of Sufism. The relations between the *imams* and the remaining Sufi communities, who against all odds continued their activities, were riddled with constant friction. For example, the Qadiriyya community met with some difficulties with the appointed *imam*, who took legal action against them for practicing obscure ceremonies forbidden by law.

The same happened to the *tekke* of the Kütahya dervishes, where the mausoleum of Ergun Çelebi is located. It was here, with some friends, that I tried to organise a *sama'* in 1992. Complaints came from the *imam* and some of the congregation of the mosque, who were outraged by the fact that we were playing music and that we dared perform the dance of the whirling dervishes there.

The *raison d'être* of this building, which had belonged to the Sufi brotherhood, had fallen into oblivion, the civil and religious authorities having taken such pains to negate it. We found a way to get round this restriction. The *tekke* included a building reserved for the *sheik* and his family. In such a 'nationalised' *tekke* it was possible to rent this private part of the building from the Ministry of Historic Monuments. In this way, certain communities managed to discreetly remain in these *tekke*. This was the case for the Uzbek *tekke*, but there, exceptionally, the entire building had been rented by Sheik Necmeddin.

Sheik Necmeddin, who was in charge of the place, found himself at the head of the community when he was still very young. During this period the 'regent' of the *tekke* was the renowned Sufi *sheik* of the Nagshbandiyya brotherhood of Istanbul, Küçük Huseyn Efendi.

The story goes that after the disappearance of the last *sheik* (Ataullah

Efendi) Sheik Necmeddin was too young to direct the community materially as well as spiritually. It was decided that he should be taken to the great Sufi master Küçük Huseyn Efendi, so that he could become his disciple and obtain the *icazet* ('certificate of aptitude') which would allow him to lead the community. Küçük Huseyn Efendi sent his representative Kudsi Efendi to take responsibility for the community. Kudsi Efendi was a very thin man, elegant, refined and very learned. It is said that he and Nafiz Uncu, another wise man of the community, went every morning for a walk in town, and on their way recited the entire Qur'an in order to refresh their memories. They chose little-used paths to avoid their recitation being interrupted by the conversations of occasional passers-by.

I myself knew Sheik Necmeddin after he had retired from the railways. At that time, he devoted himself entirely to the activities of the community. He was an astonishing man. Although he had not studied deeply he was far from ignorant, and was gifted with a great sensitivity and a wisdom that he probably owed to mixing with the people who surrounded him. His greatest satisfaction was to serve the community, and above all to enliven the weekly meetings.

Although he was not wealthy, his way of life gave the impression of a certain luxury. He had sublet a part of the building to one of his disciples who was a taxi driver. At the time, the few cars that could be seen in Istanbul were enormous Plymouths and Cadillacs. The disciple, in exchange for a reduced rent, acted as a chauffeur to the *sheik* three times a week. On Mondays, the disciple drove the *sheik* into town for supper at his son's house. On Tuesdays, he drove him to the music sessions in Göztepe and, on Fridays, to the mosque of Karaköy .

There, one could hear the most famous reciter of the Qur'an, Ali Efendi, who was a very distinguished man and, although old, gifted with a remarkable voice. But beforehand, Sheik Necmeddin would stop at a big restaurant to eat *börek*, a delicious cheese pastry, of which he would then offer 250 grams – but no more – to his chauffeur and to those who accompanied him. After attending the Friday prayers, they would go to one of the best *kebab* restaurants of Istanbul, kept by one of his disciples, and then finally to a café where they smoked the *nargile* (which the *sheik* enjoyed).He was also an inveterate cigarette smoker. The only present that the disciples who went up to the *tekke* could bring to really please him were 'Club' cigarettes, the strongest to be found in Turkey.

Once a year, Sheik Necmeddin and several chosen disciples went to Bursa, a three-hour drive from Istanbul by car. He stayed about ten days at this spa, reputed for the healing qualities of its warm waters and ancient *hammams*.

This is when he would visit a man who is still considered the greatest Sufi saint of this town: Canib Efendi. This holy man owned a house with a large garden near the Green Mosque, which was surrounded by a *bazaar* where most of the traders were his disciples. He had no children, but owned a goat of which he took uncommon care. Its horns and neck were adorned with necklaces and jewels, and it was treated just as a real human being.

In addition to this trip to Bursa, a trip to Konya took place once a year. As the *sheik* had retired from the railways, he was the one to organise the travels for the Mevlevi community of Istanbul. Two carriages were hired for the occasion. He himself selected the controller and the caterer to make the train journey as pleasant as possible. (At that time, it took two days to reach Konya.) This was an event for the whole community; the poetry and musical exchanges were extremely pleasurable. I had the good fortune to make this trip three times, and have unforgettable memories of them.

One of the characteristics of Sheik Necmeddin, who with great care supervised the proceedings of the meetings, was to give peremptory orders and sometimes even to fly into rages. He could use rude words, and call someone a 'son of an ass' or a 'pimp'. From his mouth, these insulting words seemed normal. One day, a colonel in uniform came to receive his blessing. He asked the disciples beforehand what he should do to get it. They told him, as a joke, that the *sheik's* blessing is manifested through insults. The poor colonel approached the *sheik* in the middle of a meeting with his cap under his arm and, bowing his head, said, 'Master, can you grant me a few insults?' The *sheik* always spoke his mind. He could tell someone what he really was quite frankly, and with no scruples. To the wife of a violinist from Istanbul, who came to the *tekke* from time to time, he said, after she had told him that she had dreamed of him the night before: 'I hope that, at least, you went at once to make your ablutions!'

Sheik Necmeddin knew how to create an atmosphere which, while full of humour and *joie de vivre*, never lacked in intensity or depth. He didn't care much for speeches which were too intellectual. He enjoyed listening to the Qur'an, to music or to a well-recited poem much more. He easily became angry when people showed off their knowledge in front of him.

One day, a French man came to ask him a metaphysical question: 'Can the Master explain to me the meaning of Fate?' Foreseeing a discussion far too erudite, the *sheik* took off one of his slippers, threw it at the head of the unfortunate questioner and said, 'That's your fate: to make a long journey to get a slipper thrown at your face!'

So, the learned people in the community were not in the *sheik's* good books. This was the case of Refi Cevat Ulunay, a very well-known writer who wrote for a big daily paper on literature, culture, philosophy and the arts. He was also a very talented speaker. Obviously they did not get on and, in spite of his wish, the poor journalist dared not go to the *tekke*. It was the same for Abdül Baki Gölpinarli, whose academic fame extended beyond Turkey. Gölpinarli had translated many Persian works into modern Turkish and was a recognised scholar of Sufi literature.

One can also find this attitude in Rumi, who did not appreciate the approach of the great Ibn 'Arabi to Sufism. One day, someone showed Rumi Ibn 'Arabi's great work, *Futûhât al-Makkiya* ('The Conquest of Mecca'). During the reading Rumi showed signs of being greatly bored. Luckily, a singer called Zeki came into the room. As soon as Rumi saw him he called out, 'Oh, Zeki, sing something for me. Now, enough of the *Futûhât al-Makkiya*, let *Futûhât al-Zekiya* begin!' Beyond the play on words, this signified that music was to take precedence over exegesis.

As Sheik Necmeddin did not have private means to run the *tekke*, he sometimes resorted to guile. To a financially well-off singer for whom the greatest pleasure was to perform in public, he would say, facetiously, 'If I ask you to sing once during the meeting, you must buy a sheep.' When he wished to sing a second time, the master wiggled two fingers as a sign that he should add another sheep to the first. This little teasing was also a pleasant way to provide for the needs of the community and especially for the big weekly meal. For Sheik Necmeddin, who only had his small pension to live on, it was amazing that he could receive and feed so many people every week. Never was there a meeting where food or tea was lacking. He had a kind of *baraka* where the running of the *tekke* was concerned.

My grandfather was a close friend of this *sheik* and a large photograph of him was placed next to that of the last *sheik* in the *selamlik*. One of his *neys* was always placed in a niche in the wall of this big room. From time to time, he went for a retreat for several weeks in this *tekke*.

This place was a bit like our second home. We went there every weekend, spending the night there, helping with the preparation of the big Sunday meal for the whole congregation and sometimes staying until Monday. It was quite a distance from our house to Üsküdar. Public transport was not then what it is today, so my parents, my three brothers and I had to walk, then cross the Bosphorus by boat and also climb the hill. The journey was hard, especially in winter. The road that led to the *tekke* was not asphalted and tended to become a river of mud, which often ended up in our boots.

Each week Uzbek rice was prepared, a dish composed of rice, mutton, carrots and raisins all cooked together. This tradition went back to the origin of the *tekke*. When in the seventeenth century the pilgrims from Uzbekistan settled in this place, they brought with them their traditional dish. The custom continued for almost three hundred years.

We children preferred to play in the park or go for walks in the woods between the Bosphorus and the hill rather than listen to the conversation of the grown-ups. But the time of prayer and, in the evening, the time for music were irresistible. I sometimes joined in at my father's side.

To prepare the meal or to make ourselves useful in the *tekke* was a pleasure and a joy, as was the help we brought to others outside. With the *sheik's* son and grandson, we would take some cooked rice to the police station of the district, to neighbouring houses and especially to the poor and to the taxi drivers who were queuing for the arrival of the boat. We then asked these taxi drivers to go up to the *tekke* after midnight to collect the people who had to return to their homes in Istanbul.

This great family of four or five hundred people and their children represented for me pure happiness. From these gatherings, some outstanding people remain engraved in my memory. I would like to remember some of them here, in order to pay homage to them.

One of the main characters in this *tekke* was Nafiz Uncu. In his youth, he was renowned as one of the most famous singers of Istanbul. He was the *imam* of the Yeni Cami mosque, on Üsküdar Square. Everyone in town loved his voice and would rush to listen to him recite the Qur'an or the call to prayer. He was erudite, and viewed fame as a dangerous trap. It was said that he had wished to lose his voice in order to get rid of his fame and discover again the intimate state of permanent prayer, which alone could enrich his inner happiness. God granted him his wish; when I knew him, this man's voice hardly enabled him to speak. Nafiz Uncu had a little cell at the entrance of the *tekke*. He left it only at mealtimes and went back into it immediately afterwards. On the days of the meetings, he joined in the prayer and attended the musical exchange. I have an indelible memory of him. He always leaned his head against the wall, eyes closed with radiant face, listening to the *ney* or any other instrument, to the singing and the prayers. Sometimes he let himself be taken by the ecstasy, which made him lightly tap his head against the wall. As he was always seated at the same place, the repeated tap had made a small hollow. No one dared repair it out of respect for him. This man, so kind and lovable, always had sweets in his pocket to offer us, and was a very pleasant companion.

Tufan Efendi was another remarkable person who lived in the *tekke*. *Tufan* means 'deluge' – in other words, his name was 'Mr Deluge'. His moustache, piercing look and bald head were very impressive. Tufan Efendi lived in a little cell with only a mattress on the floor and a teapot in a corner. He was known to have been a pole carrier. This trade no longer existed when I was a child. The method used involved transporting loads at the end of a wooden pole, carrying them with a certain rhythm in order to lighten the weight. He had been a well-known bandit in the Üsküdar district. There was a legend that, after a meeting with the master Nafiz Uncu, he repented and became a virtuous and erudite man. He had been allowed to live in one of the cells inside the *tekke*. Tufan Efendi was filled with regret for his misspent youth and was very sensitive to the mockery of the true believers who liked to tease him about the past. So, filled with shame, he would lower his head on his chest, which made him look even sterner than usual.

There was also Aziz Çinar, who was the *sheik* of the Arusia brotherhood. Having no other meeting place, he would gather his disciples at his home. I remember going to his house for some *zikr* or *sama'*. On Sundays, he, with all his congregation, went to the Uzbek *tekke*. He impressed us with his height, his almost completely shaven head, a huge nose above a thick moustache and dark shining eyes. He was loved and respected by his disciples who always rushed to satisfy all his wishes. Humble and unassuming, he had a fine sense of humour. As he didn't have a meeting place for his disciples, he enjoyed going to the Uzbek *tekke*.

There was a time when he could no longer gather his disciples at his house. They then met at a small café owned by one of his disciples, next to the mosque of Üsküdar. Once a week, this café would be transformed into a dervish meeting place. They practised the *zikr* ceremony; several times, I took part in it with my *ney*. On the other days of the week, the chair which was reserved for the master had to remain empty. Regular clients were careful not to sit on it – if they made this mistake, the owner would tell the ignorant man that the seat was reserved.

After a prayer and supper, we would meet in the *selamlik*. The *sheik* would then ask the musicians to play the *ney*, the *kemençe*, the *tanbur*, all instruments of the Mevlevi tradition that also belonged to 'classical music.' Sometimes Dervish Muammer, a quiet man no one really knew well, would sing Sufi poems, accompanying himself with a *mazhar* – a drum that has a frame with chains inside it. The beating of these chains on the drum skin creates a strange vibration and an extraordinary rhythmic polyphony. For hours on end, untiringly, Dervish Muammer recited or chanted poems in an ecstatic state which brought the audience to tears, to dance, overwhelmed by emotion. Thanks to some friends, I still have some recordings of that time. Just to listen to them is enough to bring back these live impressions to me. These musical moments were decisive ones for my friend Nezih Uzel and myself. The concerts and the various albums we later performed and made together in Europe came from there.

Amongst the singers and highly respected people in the Uzbek *tekke*, there was also Cevdet Soydanses, who was over ninety when he died recently. Although already old when I was young, his voice had kept a tone of remarkable quality. He was much appreciated by the master of ceremonies who, every Sunday, asked him to sing two or three songs that he particularly liked, including the following:

> *Mecnun gibi nâm istesek efsâne olurduk*
> *Sahrayi cunûn olmasa divane olurduk*
> *Birçare bulunsa mahşerde dahi*
> *Sâkini meyhane olurduk.*

> 'If like Mecnun we sought fame,
> like him we would have become a legend.
> If the Sahara of the souls did not exist
> We would have gone mad.
> If it were possible, we would take refuge
> In a tavern even at the Last Judgment.'

(*Meyhane*, here translated as 'tavern', means 'house' (*hane*) of 'wine' (*mey*). Thus the word has a double meaning in Sufi literature, 'house' and *tekke*, the place where one is filled with holy words.)

It was, as everyone agreed, one of the special moments of the evening. Later in life, I had the opportunity to question him on the history of the Uzbek *tekke* before I knew it, as well as on his memories of my grandfather.

As it was for the other *tekke* of Istanbul, a certain watchfulness was necessary to prevent the police suddenly bursting in during the ceremonies. The master had prepared a strategy: he always kept a bottle of *raki* in the fridge. This alcohol was practically considered a symbol of belonging to the Republic, so it was unthinkable for the authorities to believe that it could be drunk by 'religious fanatics'. If the police came in, the *sheik* could always bring out the bottle and say they were only having a little party amongst friends. In fact, one day plainclothes policemen appeared. The master, busy giving orders here and there for the proper running of the *tekke*, did not notice that he was ordering two representatives of the law to go down to the cellar to chop wood. The policemen, who had come to interrupt the secret gathering, found themselves – Lord knows how – chopping wood for most of the evening.

This was the only meeting place in Istanbul for the last generation of the old Sufi community. The Uzbek *tekke* no longer exists, at least not as it was originally. When I was young, the building was already falling apart. I remember as a child that the *sheik* used to tell us, when we were upstairs, to avoid jumping on the floor as it might give way at any moment and we could fall through. It goes without saying that when it rained, there were puddles here and there.

Recently, the building was restored by Ahmet Ertegün, the son of the cousin of Sheik Necmeddin. Mr Ertegün was one of the first Turkish ambassadors to the US. As an ambassador he was a strong political and cultural link between the two countries. Ahmet Ertegün and his brother Nasuhi belonged to the Turkish lobby in the US and made their fortunes there thanks to their passion for jazz. It was they who made the first recordings of the big names in jazz with the Atlantic Record Company, which they founded.

The restored building became the American Institute for Turkish Studies and, today, the son of the *sheik* is simply the caretaker. As a result of this new use, our community found itself on the street. The high society of Istanbul who attended the opening were completely ignorant of the rich and significant history of the place. Today, the Uzbek *tekke* is just an ordinary building.

In the past, the community had close links with the things that it used. For instance, there was a cupboard which was always called 'the yellow cupboard'. The master would often say, 'Go and fetch me such and such from the yellow cupboard.' I had never known it to be yellow – although it had been repainted green, it was still called 'yellow'! This small fact shows how difficult it is to keep alive the memory of a place, especially when its purpose is changed to ends which are foreign to it. I sometimes think that a ruin can better shelter the living spirit of a community than some of the most splendid palaces. The atmosphere which now reigns is almost that of a Holiday Inn. The collective memory of the community has been completely lost.

That place was the fertile soil of my formative years. My first name comes from this *tekke*, of which one of the masters was the aforementioned Kudsi Efendi. Out of respect for this man, my grandfather wished his grandson to be called 'Kudsi': 'he who belongs to the sacred'.

THREE

First Contacts with a Lay Society

In 1923, the government created state schools following the Western model. Subjects were taught in the Turkish language of course, but using the Latin alphabet. In accordance with the directives laid down by Atatürk, children from the age of five or six were instilled with a belief in a modern republic and nationalistic values. I still remember the 'credo' we had to recite every morning, standing in line two by two, whatever the weather. It began, 'I am Turkish, I am honest, I work hard' and ended with, 'What a joy to be a Turk.' We used to repeat these words, a little as in a child's game or nursery rhyme. Then, when the teacher blew her whistle we would go back, two by two, into the classrooms.

Our classrooms were rather like army barracks roofed in corrugated iron. As there were a great number of children, at least eighty pupils were crowded together in a single classroom. While this proved to be a very convenient way of keeping us warm in the winter, its drawback was the difficulty in understanding what the teacher was saying in the midst of the overall din. What I liked best, of course, was to play with my friends during the breaks.

Everything was uniform, even our clothes. We had to wear a black shirt with a white collar, like the children in the Catholic schools, with our hair in crew cuts, so that sometimes we would have fun tickling each other with our heads.

At that school, I don't remember having learned much more than the alphabet. I also remember the shouting and the slaps from the teacher. The relationship between teachers and pupils had a rather authoritarian character – entirely the opposite of what I had known in Sufi meetings where the children were treated as equals to the adults. Here, at the least outburst, we were given a thrashing. In fact, even in the street, encounters between children and adults could be rather rough.

One day, accusing me of having created havoc, the teacher got hold of my head and banged it several times on a bench. As a result, during my childhood my nose would bleed at the least provocation. When I was twelve, I had to have surgery and a vein in my nose was cauterised. The 'modern' custom of the time left the education of children to the goodwill of the teacher, which varied according to his or her mood.

Since the beginning of the nineteenth century, there were many European schools in Istanbul, most of them directed by French or Spanish Jesuit missionaries. They were intended to be for the children of foreign minorities who had settled in Turkey. Although they had lived there for several generations, most of these Europeans did not know their country of adoption. In the Italian community, many did not speak Turkish. In the Spanish community, some were Jews who had emigrated to Istanbul after the fall of Granada. They kept to themselves, and spoke not Turkish but Ladino, a dialect largely comprising Hebrew and fifteenth-century Spanish. It was through them that, at the end of the empire, the economic, commercial and political contacts with Europe were established.

Children from all these communities met in these European schools along with children from well-to-do Turkish families. My father, being a civil servant, had only a small income; I owe my entry to an Italian school to one of his friends, a former pupil of this school, who spoke so eloquently of it that in the end my father enlisted me. There, the subjects were taught in Italian. Finding myself in this school was a cultural and social shock; most of the other pupils did not speak Turkish because they were Italians or Jews, and the few Turks who went there were well-off. At first, my school results were rather good, as I was quite conscientious and sincere in my work. But I often felt a sense of disquiet in relation to my companions, due to the social and economic differences between us and the cultural approaches to the subjects we were taught. At that time, and still today, it was difficult for me to accept, in the heart of Istanbul, the study of certain pages of *The Divine Comedy* by Dante Alighieri – in particular *Inferno*, where the author relegated the Prophet Muhammad.

Amongst my friends, and even amongst my teachers, no one had the slightest idea of what a *ney* might be. When I said to those around me that my father was a musician and that he played the *ney*, I encountered only incomprehension. Little by little, I became the troublemaker of the school, the one who disturbed the quiet of the establishment. I was never at a loss to invent some new mischief. For example, in winter, nothing delighted me more than to stick a snowball to the ceiling just above the teacher's desk and to wait for it to melt. It also often happened that I played truant. All this bad behaviour was my own way of expressing my deep malaise. I completed there what is called the *scuola media*, but then, because of his illness, my father could no longer pay for me as a pupil in a private school, and so I found myself again in a state school and in a cultural environment with which I was familiar.

In the Italian school we were around fifteen pupils in a class, where now we were at least ninety. Obviously, to start with, I felt a bit lost.

The first day, from a bench behind me, I heard a pupil singing one of the compositions of my grandfather. Greatly surprised, I went to him and asked how it was that he knew that song. He replied that he had heard it very often. I proudly told him that my grandfather was the composer. To my delight, he was very impressed by that. So I found myself, at last, with some friends with whom I shared the same tastes. I was no longer alone! From then on, I could speak freely about literature and music. Amongst my friends was the son of a great artist of *tezhip* (manuscript gilding), Semih Irtes (who has followed in his father's footsteps). Another was an enthusiast for history, Necdet Içli. Today he is a well-known specialist in the historical monuments of Istanbul. With him, I would sometimes miss school in order to read works which were not suggested to us in class; for example, an account of the journey of Evliya Çelebi, a seventeenth-century author – a work of no great historical importance, but full of anecdotes and fascinating adventures. Through reading the chapter on Istanbul, we discovered the existence of a forgotten mausoleum between the ramparts of Byzantine, in the present-day quarter of Ayvan Saray.

In fact, the city of Istanbul is surrounded by the remains of two defensive walls, which stand 15 metres apart and date from the Byzantine epoch. During the first attack by the Muslims against Constantinople, many martyrs were buried there, st them the foster brother of the Prophet. In his book, Evliya Çelebi describes the mausoleum of this man and states that, at the time, the place was often visited by believers. One day, missing school, we decided to go exploring to try and discover it. We found it in a completely abandoned state. Some Anatolian peasants had settled close by. Unknowingly, they were using the approach to the mausoleum as a dump, thereby making access impossible.

We succeeded in convincing several friends and some of the people living in the neighbourhood to help us clear and restore the site. Having removed the piles of refuse, we re-installed window glass in the mausoleum and then re-erected the funerary steles scattered around the building.

Since then, and to my great astonishment, it is a place that is still visited. Whenever I am in Istanbul I never miss going there. Some women, wearing headscarves, go there to light a candle in the hope that their wish might come true, be it to find a husband, to recover their health or to be freed of the heavy misery that weighs on their shoulders.

This friend also shared with me his passion for ancient funerary steles. They were very often made of marble and had a poem inscribed, an epitaph the last words of which corresponded to the date of the death of the deceased, each of the Arabic letters representing a number. This poetic refinement brought thoughts of death, but referred also to the trade and concerns of the dead person. Istanbul is surrounded by these poems engraved in stone. This extraordinary lapidary art form reflects each epoch in its own style. At the top of each stele there is a hat or a turban, the symbol of a trade or a brotherhood. There were a great variety of hats in the Ottoman period. The uniformity of headgear came at the time of Mahmud II (1808–39) with the wearing of the *fez* (this name, which means 'Morocco' in Turkish, was given to mark its origin). Wearing this red hat was compulsory for anyone who was working as a civil servant. The expression *bachibouzouk* ('out of his mind') was used for anyone who could not be identified by his headgear: either because he was not wearing one, or because it did not correspond to the person.

With a camera, which we bought at a flea market, my friend and I started a collection of photographs. Almost every day, we went to cemeteries. There, before photographing the steles that seemed most interesting to us, we rubbed the inscriptions with chalk to bring out the calligraphy. Later, my friend met an old collector in this field, Şinasi Bey, who – as he had no heirs – presented him with his whole collection of photos. There were thousands.

A few years later, the government decided to build the ring road around Istanbul. The cemeteries were flattened. We saw, with great sadness, bulldozers lifting out the steles and dumping them into trucks which transported them Lord knows where. As fast as we could, we tried to save some of the ancient ones. We succeeded in rescuing two steles of Janissaries of the fifteenth century, as well as an old marble fountain. As we could have been accused of theft, we went undercover one night and did this with the help of a few friends, as these steles were extremely heavy.

I also had some friends who loved music. Their deep wish was to form a small band, which I would have directed. As there were already a number of Anatolian 'pop music' groups organised by the school, I went to the head of the school to ask permission to start a new group. I was faced by a man looking severe and distant. Could he be otherwise, having to supervise 5,000 pupils or more? On hearing my request, he became mad with anger and went to fetch a big book published by the Ministry of Education. He opened it, flipped over the pages with his finger, full of rage, until he found this entry, which he made me read aloud: 'Any act aiming to encourage classical Turkish music is prohibited.'

Our schoolboy dream was hitting a wall. Fortunately, during the same period, my father was visited by a young musician who had formed a group with amateurs. He had come to ask my father, as though asking permission to marry a young girl, if I could join them. The young people in the group were much older than me. Rehearsals took place once a week in the basement of a building. After a few months, we found a hall to perform in. (I must say that the audience at these concerts was mostly made up of people who had been invited by the performers themselves.)

Thanks to this meeting I heard of the existence, in the heart of Istanbul University, of a choir of classical music. This is how I found myself playing or singing classical music once a week with other students. There existed also, in the midst of another association, a group with a political tendency which wanted to reassert the value of national traditional culture. Amongst them, some were specially interested in Sufi music. All these young men considered my father as something of a living legend. I admit that I was rather proud to be the son of such a man.

Once a month, we were allowed to broadcast on the radio a programme reserved for amateur musicians. Nowadays many of them are well-known professional musicians who give concerts, teach in conservatories or are part of Broadcasting House. This was an exciting period that ended the kind of isolation I had found myself in previously. I became aware that others shared the same cultural values as those in which I had been educated.

FOUR

Traditional Music and Modernity

In Turkey, which suffered a very important cultural revolution many years before I was born, there was ambiguity in all fields. Traditional music did not escape the confusion. As religious feeling and links to Sufism were part of Ottoman culture, it was difficult for the lay authorities to give traditional music its rightful place. This very new Republic was trying to involve itself in new cultural forms, and to take European culture as a model. What the new music for this new Turkey should be was a question that arose at the very start of the Republic. The fact that Turkey belonged to an Arab-Persian civilisation with an Islamic religion was denied for the sake of joining a Western European civilisation based on Ancient Greece. But, if Ancient Greece was at the origin of this civilisation, it nevertheless had to go through a number of developing stages in order to become what it is nowadays. We Turks did not have the time to go through all these stages of evolution (at least this is what was commonly claimed by the elite). We had to catch up and assimilate at once, to obtain the beneficial effects of progress.

One means towards this was the promotion of Western classical music on national radio. In those days, just as television is now, it was an extraordinary form of communication. It was considered that, through broadcasting the music of Bach, Mozart or Chopin, it could one day be possible for composers of the same calibre to be found, even, who knows, in the remote villages of Anatolia. But this solution meant denying the whole of our true cultural, literary and musical heritage. This attempt to promote Western music and such assimilation led to the prohibition in 1937–8 of any form of traditional music. From then on, playing the *ney* or singing traditional tunes was considered to be a politically incorrect form of backward-looking attachment.

Then came the idea of raising the interest in popular music, such as it was practised in the country – in Anatolia, for instance. This music, at least, was related to our Asian past. Before the 10th century, the Turks lived in Central Asia. Popular music was more closely related to this background than the classical music which, during the Ottoman Empire, was impregnated with Arab-Persian and even Byzantine cultures. This musical heritage, rooted in popular tradition, was to become the only source of inspiration for contemporary composers. Composers such as Béla Bartók in Hungary or others in Russia and the Baltic countries succeeded in integrating these popular tunes into classical music to be interpreted by symphonic orchestras. So, in order to promote this popular musical source, researchers and musicologists were sent to Anatolia to find and transcribe live popular melodies.

Up to 1940–5 classical traditional music, such as it was played in the cultural and musical *milieu* to which my family belonged, was therefore confined to private meetings or to places called 'casinos'. In fact, they were restaurants where musicians played 'popularised' classical music. There, great masters of music would find a public. From then on a new current of thought was considered: classical music, having belonged to the Ottoman Empire, also had national-interest value. As such it deserved, just as popular music did, to become one of the sources of inspiration for contemporary composers. It was from this wish that traditional classical music was able to find its place in the national broadcast programmes.

A few passionate men such as Dr Suphi Ezgi and Hüseyin Saadeddin Arel worked on preserving the repertoire, which so far had only been transmitted orally. They had to gather the compositions from the mouths of the masters, who were often old, and transcribe them in European notation which then had to be adapted to the modal (not temperate) system used in Turkish music. My grandfather was one of the first musicians to play the *ney* at Istanbul's Broadcasting House, and then my father took his place. Unfortunately, there are only a very few recordings of them, as most of the broadcasts were live.

Broadcasting House was the source of cold, academic and soulless renditions of classical music. The difference from that which was practised in Sufi meetings was patently obvious. In the latter, there emanated a charm, a quite natural emotion, which could not be found in the broadcast concerts. This disparity seemed inexplicable: the same melodies were expressed by the same musicians in a different way. Looking back, I am tempted to explain this phenomenon by the wish, at the time, to prove that this music was noble and as great as – if not greater than – European music. Choirs were created in the European style, singing in unison but lacking the deep feeling proper to this music. The arid and cold expression came from the wish to make the music into a document, and not from the wish to have it appreciated by new generations. The enlightened music lovers, for whom music was an integral part of their cultural world, did not find it too difficult to recognise and appreciate these melodies as they had been known; but it was impossible, under the circumstances, for them to be appreciated by the young generation. Classical traditional music was condemned to become a museum piece. What was alive did not interest the authorities in the least.

Several times, I had the opportunity to accompany my father in these live broadcasts. Sitting next to the technician I was filled with emotion, and admired not only my father but also other musicians who are nowadays respected, even legendary, figures in the music world. I feel honoured to have been allowed, thanks to my father, to be in the company of the great performers of this music, which unfortunately was doomed to disappear.

The musical *milieu* in which I lived filled me with enthusiasm. There, beyond anything I could have aspired to considering my young age, I was recognised as a musician. I remember an old man, Hamdi Bey. He was a pharmacist by profession (in those days pharmacies were rare in Istanbul, and there was a certain prestige attached to this profession), and was a disciple of Kenan Rufai. He used to call me 'his *ney* player'. With my parents' agreement, he came to fetch me once a week or fortnight and took me to his house, where dinner was served with great respect by his wife. I must have been ten years old, and he must have been seventy – at least, this is how I saw him with my child's eyes. After dinner he expected me to play the *ney* for him and, as I did, he would listen to it with as much attention as if I had been a master of this instrument. The esteem I received led me to think that through imitating my father, I would one day achieve something great.

At school, in my class and sitting on the same bench, I had a friend who played the piano. One day our headmistress came into our classroom and chose my friend and me to take part in a radio broadcast of music for children. I was so overwhelmed at the thought of being asked to do the same thing as my father that I felt as though I had wings as I made my way home to bring the great news to my parents. My father made me work on three pieces. The following week, I spent whole days on these three melodies. At night, in my sleep, they haunted my dreams.

The fateful day arrived. My mother dressed me up in my best clothes. My father, holding my hand, took me to Broadcasting House. In our other hands, we each held our *neys*. Rehearsal time came; everything was absolutely ready. Then, just before the beginning of the broadcast, a man appeared. I can only remember his big belly and his suit and tie. In a rather aggressive way he took those responsible for the broadcast aside. Then and there, I did not really understand what it was all about, but very soon my father and I were made to understand that I was unwelcome and unwanted because, in those days, it was disreputable to introduce traditional classical music in a broadcast for children. What was needed, wasn't it, the argument went, was to avoid encouraging the young to fall back into an artistic form which was 'attached to the past'. Consequently, they simply showed me the door. My friend, on the other hand, was welcome because he played the piano.

This was a real shock for me, but it made me understand that I lived in two different worlds: the world of everyday life in which the *ney* had no place, and a world represented by the micro-society of traditional culture. This event also showed me that, if I wished to live my life, I had to find other values than those practised in our small community based on traditional culture. The latter did not represent society as a whole. It seemed to me that I should have other interests to share with those of my generation. This is when I begged my father to buy me an accordion. Although he was not well off he gave in to my request, and I started to have lessons with an Armenian man named Agop Pakyüz. While still being interested in the *ney*, I found in the accordion a musical form more in tune with the society outside the Sufi community, into which I had to integrate. With the *ney* I asserted my duty to perpetuate a family tradition.

FIVE

The Eye of My Father

In 1969, when he was director of the Department of Traditional Music at Radio Istanbul, my father had a visit from a well-known surgeon, Halit Ziya Konuralp. Like many doctors in Turkey, Dr Konuralp was passionate about music. He was a very proficient violinist and also enjoyed composing *şarki* (songs in classical verse). On that particular day he had brought one of his compositions for my father's appraisal.

While they were conversing, the doctor noticed that my father kept touching his face in the area of the sinuses and, on being questioned, my father remarked there was something bothering him which felt 'hard.' On hearing this Dr Konuralp persuaded my father to consult him professionally. He did so the next day at the hospital and, alas, was found to be suffering from a malignant tumour. So began a series of operations on my father's face by Dr Konuralp. Being a close friend of the family, he was invited to dine with us on the eve of the operation. After the meal, together with some other friends who were musicians, he took part in a musical evening which was like a farewell party, possibly for my father's life. The next day my father was operated on by the surgeon, the man with whom he had spent a happy evening the night before.

During a second operation my father lost an eye. At that time I played the part of the eldest son, as my elder brother was pursuing his studies in another city. It therefore often fell to me to accompany my father during his stays in hospital. I recall that when his eye was removed we did not have the courage to tell him immediately. He remained ignorant of his loss for several days. Then at dawn on the fourth day he woke up abruptly, went to the bathroom, took off his dressing and looked at himself in the mirror. The eye was no longer there! In this tragic situation my mother and I were deeply concerned about how he would react. Brushing aside our offers of help, he left his room and, unassisted, walked the length of a long corridor in the hospital. He returned, delighted, saying, 'I used the floor tiles as a guide and found I could walk in a straight line. Don't worry about me!' We had arrived at a point where it was he who was consoling us. He then told us that, the night before, Rumi had appeared to him in a dream and had told him, 'Henceforth, you will see with my eyes.' He was still under the spell of this dream when he awoke, realising at once that he had lost an eye.

In Turkish hospitals patient care is not always what it ought to be, and the help of relatives is essential in looking after patients during their stays. I often stayed at the hospital to watch over my father. One night, when I was there on my own, I took advantage of his being asleep and went down to the office-floor to smoke a cigarette (at the time I was beginning to smoke, and smoking in front of one's elders was not done). It so happened that I went into a room and saw a wall covered with shelves full of jars containing various organs that were intended for use in teaching at the medical school. On one of the labels I could read the words 'right eye of Mr Erguner'. It was a terrible shock to see my father's eye in a jar. When I returned to his room he saw from my face that something had upset me, and asked what had happened. As he insisted, I felt obliged to tell him what I had seen. He responded with a broad smile and said, 'Listen! I just don't understand. When you were a child and misbehaved I used to look at you sternly, and it didn't touch you at all, and now, you see this dead eye in a jar and you are afraid?!' This comment from my father shocked me deeply.

During the time I spent with my father while he was in hospital having a succession of operations, I found myself in other strange situations. I often had the opportunity to help and to keep company with the patients who occupied the neighbouring rooms. I particularly remember one old man to whom, each day, his children brought blankets, as he constantly complained of being cold. His daughter would carefully lay them all out on his bed and ask me, when I was spending the night there, to make sure I kept watch to see that her father stayed well-covered. Then, one night, this man died, and it was left to his daughter to wheel his body to the hospital's cold room. How strange life can be!

At that time I was seventeen years old, and finding life full of strong experiences that were very enriching on a personal level. During the day I worked at Broadcasting House with very talented musicians. Once a week I played in various *tekke* in Istanbul. There was also a weekly gathering of great masters of music who met in a café and smoked their *nargiles*. I went there on my own, or accompanied by my father when his health permitted. I was very close to people of my father's generation and, thanks to the groups of amateurs with which I played, I was also able to share my passion with those of my own generation.

While he was the director of the music section at the Broadcasting House in Istanbul, my father was in a position to meet people who wished to entrust him with documents related to traditional music. These texts proved to be very precious in the perpetuation of that knowledge. This is how, one day, he was visited by a learned man who lived as a hermit in a cell of the mosque in Eyüp. This man had four books of music written in *Hamparsum*, a classical Turkish music notation, which he had inherited from his master. As he was already rather old and had no one to give them to, he wished to leave them to my father. He gave him all his papers with much love and humility when we went to see him in his cell.

There was also a *ney* player, Hasan Dede, to whom we paid a visit. He was a very cultivated man, out of the ordinary, who lived a solitary life. There was also a *sheik* from Sarajevo, who had emigrated to Istanbul with all his family. A whole community settled in Istanbul around my father.

The visits of these men showed the extent to which the musical and literary heritage of the Ottoman Empire had left traces awaiting to be revealed. Whatever did become known was probably only a very small sample of the hidden treasures. Years later I discovered, piled up in a heap and hidden from sight in the vaults of the mosque of Yeni Cami on Usküdar Square, all the material seized from the *tekke* when the Sufi meetings became forbidden. In this damp underground these venerable relics, including flags, books, clothes and musical instruments, were left to rot. My begging was of no avail, and none of it could be saved.

As for my father, for nights on end he threw himself into transcribing the compositions that were brought to him into European notation. He would then ask me to interpret them on the *ney*, in order to correct them. So I had the good fortune to be the very first to learn, feel, and interpret these pieces.

Because of the loss of his eye, my father found it difficult to read. His pain kept him awake at night, and often he would ask me to read to him. Thanks to this situation, from very early on I had a knowledge of Sufi texts and history books, uncommon for young men of my age. I spent long nights in his company, reading, playing the *ney* or simply talking with him. Once, around 3 AM, he woke me up, having just finished transcribing a composition by al-Farabi . He called to me: 'Come, come and play this!' This is how I was able to profit from the great knowledge and experience of this man who had so much to teach, and who shaped my passion for music.

These moments remain deeply engraved in me. They are a part of the teaching I received, either in words or by the example of his attitude to life. My father made me understand that, having been taught music and the *ney* free of charge, no matter who the pupil was, when I found myself in the position of teaching I would have to do so without asking for payment. He also made it clear that the *ney*, such a venerable instrument, was not an instrument that could be sold. I have respected this advice and, although I have had many pupils, I have never asked to be paid for teaching music or for providing a *ney*.

Another example will illustrate how strictly he followed this principle. One day a young man from Konya came to our house with a tape recorder. He was in the process of starting a record company and wanted to make his first record with my father who, to this end, improvised four pieces on the *ney*. On his way out, the young man discreetly left an envelope in the cloakroom. My father, realising this, said to me: 'This man must have left this money. Since he is starting a business, he needs it more than I do! Run after him and give it back to him!' I ran out into the street and gave him back his envelope. With these four recordings, the young man was able to start a successful record company in Konya. Although I have not always been able to observe such high principles, these attitudes have been, for me, examples of proper action and uprightness.

When I was at the Italian school, I sometimes played truant and took boat trips on the Bosphorus. I wanted just as much to escape from the harsh reality of school life as to admire the reflection of the autumn colours on the water. By the end of the first term at school, I had already missed twenty days. My father learned of my regular absence from lessons. One day, he came to fetch me from school. Almost smiling, and not saying a word about my absences, he asked me if all was well and if I didn't sometimes play truant. I answered, very casually, that all was well. Then he asked, 'Why are you lying?' I blushed, wishing I could disappear underground. I was expecting to be punished, or at least severely reprimanded. He looked at me sternly and told me to follow him. Having walked a short way, he took me to a pastry shop. Dryly, he told me to sit down at a table, and then he ordered an iced cake, which I ate in silence. Then, he ordered a second one, and said to me: ' From now on, every time you do something silly in your life, you'll come here and eat a cake on my behalf and you'll think of me.' This was my only punishment, and it certainly left a greater mark than the one I was expecting. Nowadays, every time I go to Istanbul, I go to this same pastry shop and order the same cake – let's say, as a precaution!

SIX

The Whirling Dervishes
Ceremonies in Konya

Until the Fifties, the Turkish laws aimed at the transformation of society were very strictly applied. In 1950, after thirty-seven years of Republican leadership, the success of the Democratic Party began a period of shared power which lasted until 1960. The lack of sincerity of the politicians did not seem to matter; the new party benefited from the excesses of the preceding period, notably those with a fascist tendency, and this helped it to gather the support of the working class.

The call to prayer is a significant example. In the whole of the Muslim world it is always made in Arabic, the language of the Prophet. In 1938, the government ruled that it should be made in Turkish, in order to 'nationalise' the religion of Islam. The Democratic Party promised a return to the call to prayer in Arabic, which the people warmly welcomed. This fact, as well as other measures more in keeping with the social situation in Turkey, brought them power. In 1960, the army could no longer tolerate these examples of liberalism, which contradicted the aims of the founders of the Republic. It came to power in a *coup d'état*, and the leader of the Democratic Party was hanged.

As for the Sufis, this brief relaxed period made it possible to organise commemorative ceremonies in Konya . They started in 1956. Following the Marshall Plan, Turkey received help from the US, which was as much military as economic and, in particular, consisted of food. I myself belonged to the generation that was brought up on powdered milk and cod liver oil, which were supposed to give us strength and which were supplied by the Americans. An official delegation of American diplomats and army officers came to Turkey to ascertain how efficiently the help was being provided. In Konya, when they came to visit the mausoleum of Celâleddin Rumi, the wife of one of the official delegates enquired about the dervishes. The Turkish officials who were acting as guides to these esteemed hosts were thrown into a panic. They had to find dervishes to introduce to them without delay. A few musicians were called upon to organise a Sufi ceremony. My father, who was a civil servant in Ankara at the time, was amongst those who were asked, as was Halil Can, a *ney* player, Saadeddin Heper, venerated as the last player of *kudum* in the *tekke* of Pera in Istanbul, and a few others. (The *kudum* is a percussion instrument made from a pair of small cups, whose dry, dull sound resembles the hammering of metal in the Konya *bazaar* which gave Rumi the inspiration for the dance of the future whirling dervishes.)

The mayor of Konya thought that this initiative, which was due to special circumstances, could be of interest. The following year, he organised a ceremony to commemorate Rumi's passing. The anniversary corresponded that year to the 17th of December, according to the Islamic calendar. Henceforth, this date was kept for all the yearly commemorative ceremonies, without any notice being taken of the disparity between the lunar and solar calendars. This decision created some friction between the mayor, who was elected by the Democratic Party, and the governor of the province, who was nominated by the government. The following year it was decided that the ceremony should take place in the basketball stadium in Konya. When the news arrived in Istanbul, it created a real turmoil in the Sufi brotherhood. Who would participate, and what costumes would they wear?

In Kenan Rufai's community (he himself had died, and one of his favourite disciples, Mrs Ayverdi, had succeeded him), they began to make costumes for the dervishes. Everyone was moved, reminded of the good old days when it was not necessary to practise the ceremony in secret.

Contrary to what is believed nowadays, Konya did not have much to do with the dervishes. Apart from Rumi's mausoleum, neither in Rumi's time nor later did the town have any special relationship with the members of the Sufi community. During the Ottoman Empire there were about 110 centres – in Athens, Cyprus, Crete, Cairo, Damascus, Jerusalem. There were five in Istanbul, all under the authority of a descendant of Rumi who was surrounded by a committee of wise men called *dede*. They resided in Konya, close to Rumi's mausoleum; but Konya was not, strictly speaking, a dervish centre.

Without going into the details of the dervish influence on the history of Ottoman culture, it is worth remembering that this community played an important part from the sixteenth and seventeenth centuries until the fall of the empire. *Sultans*, as well as poets and musicians, were disciples of Rumi and belonged to one or another *tekke* in Istanbul. In spite of trials and tribulations, the school of dervishes survived through these centuries.

As there were no dervishes in Konya itself, those from Istanbul were called upon to organise the ceremonies for what was later called the Konya Festival. That year, a special train was hired for the several hundred people who were to take part. A large number of representatives from various Sufi brotherhoods gathered from all over the country to participate in this historical event. The governor of the province told them that the festival was not meant to be anything more than a folklore performance. He warned them that they could get into serious trouble if the ceremonies were enacted in the spirit of authentic Sufi rituals. This was a paradox bordering on absurdity: on the one hand, an opportunity not to be missed at any cost and on the other, the impossibility of performing this ceremony in a truly religious way.

These few years when the Turkish Sufi communities as a whole (and not only the Mevlevi dervishes) could gather together, were the golden age of these ceremonies.

After the military coup in 1960, the army officers decided to attend the ceremonies. At that time, three people were responsible for their organisation. These were Mithat Bahari, a great commentator on Rumi's *Mesnevî* and whose teachings I followed; he was assisted by two other *sheiks*, Resuhi Baykara and his older brother Gavsi Baykara, both sons of the last *sheik* of Yeni Kapi, the largest Mevlevi centre in Istanbul. The ceremony started in the presence of the generals-in-chief, trailed by the television crew. Now, even though the ritual was presented in a sports hall, the very presence of the *sheik* made it a sacred ground. Traditionally, people who were not participating in the ceremony were not allowed to enter the space where it took place.

Here, a mockery was being made of the tradition – photographers and television cameramen entered the hall and started filming the whirling dancers. One of the three *sheiks*, Resuhi Baykara, unable to bear the situation, became enraged and chased out the intruders. All this was taking place in front of the general-in-chief, Cemal Gürsel, who had instigated the coup. It caused a real scandal.

From then on, it was decided in high places that the Sufi community of Istanbul should no longer be invited. As they wished, in spite of it all, to safeguard the festival, they found Ahmet Bîcan Kasaboglu, who was almost the lowest in the hierarchy of dervishes in Istanbul. He offered to teach the whirling dance of the dervishes to young men in Konya. Advertisements were put in local papers to recruit schoolboys and teach them the *sama'* in preparation for the following year's ceremonies. Those who presented themselves were accepted according to criteria based on their size, the beauty of their faces and how well they moved. Most of them belonged to the town's football or basketball teams. Under Bîcan Kasaboglu's direction, they learned to 'whirl' in a few months. Then they were dressed up in costume and *sikke* (felt hat), which made them look like dervishes.

The following year, there was an outcry in Istanbul. I remember it well because many decisions regarding the situation were made in meetings at my father's house. What to do? Were the musicians, indispensable elements in the practice of the *sama'*, to participate in this parody of the ritual? There was no one in Konya with the sensitivity, skill and understanding required to do justice to the musical part of the ceremony. After a number of discussions, it was decided to continue to play for the *sama'* in order to have at least some control over what was happening in Konya.

As the authentic community of whirling dervishes was being discredited and once again forced to go underground, each year the ceremonies in Konya were tending more and more to folklore. Nowadays, too many people interested in Sufism or dervishes have no doubt that Konya is the great centre for this mystical movement. This is wrong. Konya took hold of a tradition and transformed it into an object of folklore. In 1967 there was an attempt to expel the musicians who came from Istanbul, just as with the dancers a few years earlier, and replace them with musicians trained in Konya.

The Department of Tourism was in charge of all these activities. It had been founded and was directed by a young lawyer, Feyzi Halici, who later became a senator. At the ceremonies, he had the terrible habit of making speeches that lasted longer than the ceremony itself. A letter was sent to my father, and to others responsible in the community, informing them that henceforth the town of Konya would no longer require their services, as the music for the *sama'* was being entrusted to local musicians. Musically, this was a catastrophe.

Since the beginning of the Republic, each town, as in Europe, had its own brass band. The authorities in Konya decided to call on their band to interpret the music of the dervishes. The band consisted mainly of retired military musicians. Dressed in their richly coloured outfits, they would give an open-air concert in front of the sports hall, after which they would quickly go in and change clothes – better to say dress up – as Sufi musicians. The result was so terrible that the authentic musicians from Istanbul were, once again, called upon. After many discussions within the community, it was decided by my father and Saadeddin Heper to accept a return to Konya.

The town of Konya shelters a very religious if not orthodox population. It tended to become a centre of attraction for people of all nations who were interested in Sufism and the Mevlevi tradition. At first, the audience consisted essentially of members of authentic Sufi brotherhoods, but from the Seventies, it became Westernised. Our first trips to the West prompted many Europeans, who wished to find the source of what they practised in London or Paris, to go to Konya. One could meet Sufis from California or New York, mystics from Paris, followers of Gurdjieff ; and all sorts of people versed to various degrees in mysticism. They came in coach-loads, and watched the ceremonies with an interest that had been sharpened by their respective spiritual guides. On the other hand, with many musicians of *sama'* being strangers to Konya since they came from Istanbul, more opportunities for meaningful meetings existed. The atmosphere was rather paradoxical, because although those who actually practised the whirling dervish dances often knew almost nothing about them, sometimes in the audience there were erudite Europeans with a lot more knowledge of the Mevlevi tradition.

The welcoming people of Konya, as well as the city being an environment rich in religious history, corresponded very well with the Oriental-mystic image formed in European minds. It was, nevertheless, a meeting of the European mystic-image with a ritual performance completely emptied of its meaning, however aesthetically pleasing it may have been.

Contrary to the Europeans, who had come earlier and who belonged to a certain intellectual *milieu*, in 1973 we saw the arrival of the young Californian 'baba cool' type in quest of mysticism. This had a tremendous effect on the youth of Konya, triggering a real explosion where individual freedom was concerned. Men and women's relationships, which until then obeyed very strict rules, were suddenly open to question. The young dervish dancers, mixing with Californian girls without any inhibitions, behaved in a way previously unthinkable. There was uproar in the town, and people were so deeply troubled that some of the most orthodox made attempts on the lives of others.

In Konya, the festival was becoming a media event in the very heart of Turkey. The presence of the head of state and his prime minister was widely broadcast. It was an occasion for them to show their goodwill towards the people. They used the festival as a platform for their speeches. Meanwhile, we had to wait for hours behind the stage. We had to use much persuasion to convince the authorities to cease these irrelevant intrusions.

In this short history of the contemporary whirling dervishes, the part played by Celâleddin Rumi, a descendant of Rumi who died in 1996, must also be mentioned. Until that time, he had remained largely unknown. He lived in Antakia, and business was his main occupation. In spite of the fact that he was Rumi's descendant, until then he took absolutely no interest in the whirling dervishes. When he retired, he went to live in Istanbul and, remembering his illustrious ancestry, he decided he wanted to manage the activities of the whirling dervishes. They were becoming more and more important on a national as well as international level. In his view, it was unthinkable to allow this organisation to grow in an anarchic way.

Celâleddin Çelebi's name can be added to the list, already quite long, of those who spoke endlessly before the start of the ceremony at the Festival of Konya. Having spent his childhood in the city of Aleppo in Syria when it was under French rule, he could speak French perfectly . This gave him a further trump card, which enabled him to present himself as the expert who should master all Sufi activities. From 1977, Saadeddin Heper, my father and other musicians were no longer there and everything was in the hands of Feyzi Halici. The latter helped to make the Festival of Konya into nothing more than a manifestation of folklore.

The 'eso-touristic' influx of the Seventies corresponded with the trip we made to Europe.

SEVEN

The First Tours of the Whirling Dervishes Outside Turkey

As early as 1968, the first tours in Europe gave rise to many discussions within the community as to their relevance. The decisions were made by those at the top of the Sufi hierarchy, after discussions that had been open to all.

There were different views. For the *ney* player Halil Can, to perform the *sama'* in Europe was an important event, but it had to be done by true initiates. For others, on the other hand, it was better to show the young dancers of Konya, who were more attractive in the way they moved, and who corresponded better to the idea Westerners might have had of the whirling dervishes.

These tours also risked strong criticism by the Western-minded in the government who did not take kindly to Turkish people projecting a 'retrogressive' image of Turkey abroad. This could result in serious retaliation against the Sufi brotherhoods. In 1968, it was nevertheless decided to accept an invitation by UNESCO to organise a ceremony in Paris. This event was well-received.

I had the honour of participating in the second performance, which took place in 1970 at the Théâtre de la Ville. During a festival of whirling dervishes, the son of the deputy mayor of Konya met a young French architect, Hervé Baley, who was interested both in Frank Lloyd Wright and, in a different way, in G. I. Gurdjieff, a spiritual seeker who died in 1949 and whose followers considered a master with a gift for making mystical Eastern teachings accessible to Westerners. Hervé came several years in a row to Konya. His interest in what he saw there led him to become one of our first European contacts. The deputy mayor's son, who was living in Hervé's house while studying in Paris, arranged a meeting on his own initiative with the director of the Théâtre de la Ville and signed a contract for seven performances of the whirling dervishes. As far as the arrangements were concerned, the contract was not very professional.

A coach to Paris was hired from Konya via Istanbul, where the musicians boarded. The trip was a real odyssey. The coach was packed full and, being rather past its prime, took nearly a week to reach Paris, during which time we ate tins of beans and stuffed vine leaves which we had stocked up in the luggage hold. First we crossed Bulgaria, at that time under communist rule. To us it seemed a phantom country. In the towns, the streets seemed deserted and the roads were extremely poor. However, in the villages we passed through, the atmosphere was hardly any different to those in Turkey. It was the same in the south of Yugoslavia, where the imprint of Ottoman culture was present everywhere. Many of the people, police or customs officials with whom we had dealings spoke Turkish. We had the feeling that we had not really left our own country.

Once we had left Belgrade, we began to feel that we had reached Europe and one night, very suddenly, we found ourselves in West Germany. As the journey was rather trying for the older members of the group, we decided to stop in Munich and eat some good hot soup at a Turkish restaurant, of which we knew there were many in the country. We got completely lost in this foreign city and were quite unable to find a single Turkish restaurant. Having wandered the streets for a long time, at last we came across a man who did not look like a German. He wore a very full moustache and, much to our joy, turned out to speak our language. Unfortunately, although we had fallen into the hands of a fellow countryman, he must have been one of the local villains. No doubt seeing a good business opportunity, and mistaking us for common tourists out for a good time, he led us not to a restaurant as we had requested but to a sleazy bar full of drunks and women of, let us say, 'easy virtue'. I will never forget the sight of our old Sufi master, deeply alarmed and heading back to the coach at full speed.

The Turk who had led us there was rather disappointed by our disapproving attitude. We succeeded nevertheless in persuading him to guide us out of the city, as night had fallen. He and two of his friends led us to the motorway, at the wheel of a superb Mercedes. They stopped at the slip road, got out of the car and brought out guns from inside their jackets; then all three began shooting into the air. It was their way of wishing us a good journey. This was the strange start that marked our first contact with Europe.

We finally arrived in Paris that week. There, we settled in a small hotel behind the Panthéon in the heart of the Latin Quarter and close to the Châtelet, where the performances were due to take place. Our material situation was most precarious. Each one of us had been allowed 100 *francs* for food for the whole week, during which seven performances were to be given. It proved to be quite a challenge! The young dancers from Konya were disappointed, but, even worse, some of them actually fainted in the evening for lack of food. Moved by our conditions, Hervé Baley opened his house to the forty or so members of the group, and he and his partner Daniel Ginat offered us the use of their office. We are still grateful to them for it! However, at the time, this generosity seemed obvious to us, as in Istanbul to keep an open table for 100 people was nothing exceptional. Looking back, I now realise how extraordinary their hospitality was, considering we were in Europe.

It is hard to convey how much Paris fascinated us. But we had not imagined that in Paris people lived more or less in the same way as those in Istanbul. They seemed just as warm, and certain aspects of their character and of their culture did not feel all that foreign to us; but after all, hadn't Turkey been profoundly influenced by French culture since the eighteenth century? We saw the similarities more than the differences.

We especially noticed the beauty of the women, which was enhanced by an exquisite elegance and also a kind of sophistication which seemed to govern the relationships between people. The city itself impressed us with the beautiful stone apartment buildings of the Haussmann epoch, as we only knew the crumbling remains of an empire and the ruins of timber houses, all in a jumble of urban disorder. Proud as Istanbul is entitled to be of its rich history and beautiful setting, it is spoiled by its chaotic town planning. But above all, in Paris the architecture and the monuments gave us an impression of joy which celebrated the past as well as the present.

Consumer society displayed its wealth before our astonished eyes, and the attraction was difficult to resist. We spent most of our free time looking for presents to bring home to our loved ones. Fortunately, anticipating such purchases, most of us had brought some modest savings. The department stores made one dizzy with the abundance of goods on display, which in no way corresponded to what we were used to finding at home. It was like a surging tide after a dam has burst. I had, at once, the feeling that it was necessary to protect myself from this phenomenon, for it was evident that this mass of objects no longer had any relation to usefulness. Until then we had lived very simply, satisfying just our essential needs. Here were objects, displayed everywhere, feeding the imagination while absolutely unrelated to any need. I never imagined then that these superfluous objects would one day become, for the Europeans as for the Turks, goods considered absolutely indispensable for one's happiness. The ingenious spirit of commerce knew how to make these accessories so necessary. In the evening, back at the hotel, each of us proudly showed off his finds. This buying fever was such that no one on the coach returning to Istanbul had a penny in his pocket.

The ceremonies we performed at the Théâtre de la Ville were a success. After each performance, a good 100 people stayed behind in the hall to meet us and find out more about our traditions. Everything went very well. As for the Turkish embassy officials, they had little interest in our activities, which reminded them too much of what they were trying to keep hidden in Turkey. The only welcome we received from them came through the Office of Tourism, located on the Avenue de l'Opéra, which considered us a folk group. They gave a reception in our honour, but we had been invited for such a late hour that when we arrived the buffet had been cleared. The organisers had delayed our arrival on purpose, fearing a lack of *savoir-faire* on our part. Thinking we were ignorant peasants, they probably expected us to eat with our fingers. Since our supposed lack of manners was not in accord with the distinguished presence of diplomats and respectable people, it had been thought more reasonable to limit the damage by inviting us when there was nothing left to eat.

In the end, in spite of the difficult money problems and the hard journey, we were more than delighted by our stay in Paris. We had more than enough time to share our feelings about it during the return coach trip, which was more trying still than the outbound one. We were all in agreement that it was neither a financial nor a missionary interest that had guided our steps (it never crossed our minds that one day the French would transform themselves into adepts of our brotherhood), but it was rather the pure joy of having created a goodwill, an understanding and a respect for our tradition that we were far from finding at home. We had not travelled this 3,000-kilometre journey under such difficult conditions in vain: it had allowed us to breathe an atmosphere in which we finally felt alive.

Many years later, I realised that the French then imagined that we had come straight from a monastery, from a traditionally organised *tekke*. This was far from the truth. If the men still existed, the places themselves no longer did. After the disappearance of the older generation, the guardians of the tradition, even the men became invisible. As the new generation did not have the benefit of a specific transmission of traditional knowledge, the activities of the whirling dervishes fell into profane hands.

The following year, we went to London for the first time, by air. For most of us, who had never thought of taking a plane, the prospect of such a trip had been as remote as a rocket journey to the moon would have been for a European. Anyone travelling by plane was then considered to be a daredevil, with courage to be admired. Every member of the community was accompanied by his whole family to Istanbul airport, which at the time was not very big. There was great emotion at the departure, with much waving of handkerchiefs.

Our welcome in London was unlike that which we had received a year ago in Paris. Whereas it was the cultural aspect that seemed to interest the Parisians, in London the interest was above all in the religious, even spiritual side of our brotherhood. There were a great number of established spiritual or religious communities in this city, and some of them saw us as a means of bringing them closer to the mystical East they had heard about from their *gurus*.

We were welcomed with open arms by members of the Gurdjieff groups, as well as by another group originating with P. D. Ouspensky, which met in a large building called Colet House. Their leader was a Dr Roles. After Gurdjieff's death, some of his disciples had gone to Turkey, where they discovered the whirling dervishes. They saw a connection between these dances and the sacred dances taught by Gurdjieff . As the master was no longer alive, they thought that they would find with the Sufis a way to pursue the spiritual teaching to which they aspired. With this in mind, they had separated from the original group, which continued to believe in the validity of Gurdjieff's teachings even after his death.

Dr Roles and some of his disciples, having decided to follow the Sufi way, opted for the teaching of the whirling dervishes. To do this, they went to see the son of the last *sheik* of Yeni Kapi, Resuhi Baykara. For the first time, the question arose as to whether it was possible to be initiated to Mevlevi Sufism without being a Muslim, as there are four stages on the path: *shari'a* (Islamic law, including strict respect for the Qur'an and the traditions of the Prophet); *tariqa* (the 'way'); *hakikat* (the 'truth'); and *ma'rifat* (the 'knowledge'). The first, *shari'a*, did not apply to non-Muslims. However, the *sheik* accepted to teach them the *sama'*, although the Mevlevi brotherhood of Istanbul was not in accordance.

Although we thought we were only going to perform the ceremony in an ordinary hall, we were rather surprised to find ourselves in a *tekke* such as there had been in our country fifty years before. The members of the community were dressed in the traditional dervish costume and danced in a true *sama'* hall. As for us, members of the Sufi community of Istanbul, who endlessly questioned whether it was possible for Europeans to understand our music, we were witnessing people practising the ceremony – and, furthermore, in a real *tekke*.

The *Mesnevî*, translated by R. A. Nicholson, was read aloud and listened to in a meditative state. This preceded the *sama'*, which was generally accompanied by taped music. That day, we performed the musical part of the ceremony.

The meetings with the 'orthodox' Gurdjieff groups were also very intense. We did not go to their centre, but met in the vast basement of an art gallery specialising in icons owned by a young aristocrat, Richard Temple. In the evening, after the ceremony, he welcomed the performers and members of the Gurdjieff groups. There we played some music, which was listened to with great attention, or we did a *zikr*. Through music and conversation, every evening was an occasion for serious contact.

To be able to practise the ritual of the whirling dervishes in England and to be respected by these Europeans (or at least by those who belonged to the circles with which we had contact), when it was prohibited by our own government, seemed to us the height of absurdity. What seemed especially absurd was the fact that we were discovering a kind of world that the government of our country wanted to impose on us, while this world was doing all it could to identify itself with our cultural traditions.

During our third journey, there were two unfortunate events within the company directed by my father. Amongst the musicians were two *ney* players, Selami Bertug and Niyazi Sayin, old pupils of my grandfather. They were not really part of the Sufi community but, because of their fame in Turkey, which was well deserved, my father decided to include them in the company. These men tried to make him wear a dinner jacket for the ceremonies in order to present a more 'modern' image of Turkey. When he refused, they threatened to report him to the relevant Turkish authorities. Niyazi Sayin also took the liberty, at the opening of the ceremony, to play an arrangement for the *ney* of a work by Bach. In his mind, this absurdity would heighten the appreciation of European audiences.

The following year, when I brought my father back to London so that he could follow a course of radiotherapy, I found unfailing help and support amongst the members of the various London Sufi brotherhoods. I became aware of the authenticity of their way: they did not just dress as dervishes once a week, but they had in their daily life a just and human attitude. These interesting meetings, where we talked and played music, were made possible by the presence amongst us of several authentic Sufi musicians.

The language barrier was a handicap for most of us. The exceptions were Nezih Uzel, a disciple of the Uzbek *tekke,* journalist and graduate of the French Lycée, and Cinuçen Tanrikorur, an *oud* player who had learned French. The latter, even though he was an accomplished musician, had little knowledge of Rumi or Sufi teachings in general. The Europeans admired him as an Eastern musician who was spiritually advanced. He took the French whom he met to be extremely intelligent people, while for him, the East was full of nothing but fools. Nezih Uzel had been brought up in the Sufi teachings, but he did not want to follow the example of Sheik Necmeddin, who liked to give learned talks. In England, contact was made possible thanks to one of Kasaboglu's students, Nail Kesova, who had mastered our language. There again, the connection was made on the basis of music and on human relationships, which opened the way to more profound exchanges. But communication was essentially through music.

During these journeys certain events occurred which went against our tradition. We had to be very attentive to our behaviour, which had to be exemplary even when we were not in dervish costume performing the ceremonies. As Rumi said: 'It is necessary to be as one appears', or 'it is necessary to appear as one is.' Sufism is a *tariqa*, a way, the source of which is in Islam, and according to which the drinking of alcohol is forbidden. In the history of Mevlevia there is no record of *sama'* being practised in a state of drunkenness. But, during the meetings at Hervé Baley's house, Bîcan Kasaboglu (who had become an important person through teaching dervish dancing to the young men of Konya) started drinking wine and whisky, to excess. Under the influence of the music as much as the alcohol, he started to perform the *sama'*, upsetting everything around him in the process. This, alas, sadly took place in the presence of the greatly respected Saadeddin Heper.

In 1972 we made our very first journey to the US, thanks to Mrs Carlways, an influential person who liked to encourage the American public to share discoveries she considered interesting in the fields of theatre or music. During a visit to Konya, she had been impressed by the ceremony of the whirling dervishes. On her return she organised a grand tour for us. My father, though already seriously ill, was encouraged by the members of the community to lead the group. This also gave him the possibility of being examined by American doctors, and of trying to find a cure for the illness that was consuming him. In New York, Chicago, Los Angeles, San Francisco and Seattle we were welcomed in the largest halls.

I still have lively memories of New York. There we met Pir Vilayat Khan, the head of the International Sufi Movement. We saw their 'mystical Sufi' dances. It was a surprise for us to see men and women practising a ceremony together. These dances borrowed certain elements of the *sama'* such as we practised at home, but here they were transformed into something else. On a human level, the attitude of these American mystics towards us was full of true devotion, as if we were saints. They greatly overestimated us!

In New York and elsewhere, we met many people who belonged to the Gurdjieff groups, as well as to other groups. Very often, after the performances, we were received by members of these various communities. I remember one in particular, which comprised several thousand young disciples. It was led by a man with an impressive beard who called himself 'Sufi Sam'. These thousands of young disciples lived communally, as though in a real village, in the very heart of San Francisco.

Our stay in Los Angeles was most turbulent. We had been warned that anti-Turkish demonstrations were being organised by the Armenian community. At the entrance of the hall where the performance was to take place Armenians, shouting and waving flags, tried to prevent us from entering. The atmosphere was tense, to say the least. We were nevertheless able to go onstage and start the ceremony. Suddenly, people in the audience started to shout in unison. At the time we did not understand what it was all about; in fact, they were rhythmically intoning, roughly, *Insh'allah mabu dela* ('If God wishes, He is the only One to love'). The pronunciation was so different from ours that we were far from understanding what was happening. We were rather worried, as we all had in mind the possibility of an interruption by the Armenians. In fact, the disciples of the International Sufi Movement had come in large numbers and wished to welcome us in a way they thought appropriate.

Soon after, some American policemen invaded the stage and stopped the dervishes as though the latter were tops, silenced the music and cleared the hall: there had been a bomb alert. We were obliged to return to our hotel under police escort. A uniformed man was placed outside each of the doors to our rooms. This situation continued throughout our stay in Los Angeles. This tour greatly contributed to the influx of American 'eso-tourism' in Turkey.

EIGHT

In London, then Paris

Our stay in London had given the opportunity to my father and me to make authentic contacts with certain circles interested and active in the field of Sufism. Several people offered to help my father to find specialists in the disease that afflicted him. Thanks to this support, it was decided that we would return to the British capital the following year so that he could be hospitalised. Our Turkish friend and surgeon had advised us to consult a professor at Hammersmith Hospital, where it would be possible to consider radiotherapy treatment. Just as we had abandoned all hope, we were told that the Turkish government – during a ministerial cabinet meeting and as proposed by our doctor – had agreed to meet all hospital expenses. As it was necessary for me to accompany him, some family jewellery was sold to cover the cost of my stay and to repatriate my father's body if, by misfortune, he died during his treatment in England. Thus, one grey winter day in 1972, we went to Istanbul's airport together with a crowd of friends and neighbours. We sadly felt that behind their encouragement and wishes for his recovery was a goodbye.

It was not the first time I had flown, but never had a plane seemed so cold and metallic as during this journey, and the dark clouds covering my thoughts were not of a kind that could be surpassed by altitude. With my family and friends left far behind me, the responsibility I was to assume weighed heavily on my young shoulders.

Upon our arrival, a pleasant surprise awaited us. We were greeted by the smiling and friendly face of Annette Courtenay and her husband Dr Bernard Mayers, from the London Gurdjieff Society. Although we had written to both of them to announce our arrival, we were far from expecting that they would greet us at the airport like members of their own family. They had prepared a room in their home for my father until he could be admitted to the hospital. It is difficult to describe the feelings we experienced in the face of such a gesture. Here we had proof that certain human attitudes were not the sole prerogative of a given tradition or religion, but could be found anywhere human beings exist.

Some days later my father entered the hospital. We took him there, accompanied by Paul Keller (director of the 'World of Islam' exhibition), together with the Indian musician Mahmud Mirza. Dr Mayers introduced me to one of his friends, Robert Browne, an art restorer and painter who had travelled in Turkey and spoke Turkish. Some years before, he had travelled there for a few months with only a few pennies in his pocket. In those days tourism was not as developed as it is today and, with the hospitality of Turkish villagers, he did not even need to spend the little money he had. For him, our stay in London was an opportunity to repay what had been offered to him by a whole nation. He had a large workshop and flat near Oxford Circus and, as he was a bachelor, it was decided that I would stay with him. In spite of our having little in common, this was the start of a long friendship. He loved whisky, whereas I could not take the smallest drop of alcohol; he was a bohemian at heart, while I preferred an orderly lifestyle; he was a follower of the Gurdjieff teachings, about which I was able to learn a little more during our lengthy nocturnal discussions.

Early each morning, I went to the hospital by Underground and arrived before the doctor's round. I was able to act as an interpreter between my father and his doctors, as my conversations with Robert had helped me to make noticeable progress in the English language. Usually I stayed with my father until the end of visiting hours. Because he had a private room, I could sometimes hide myself there until the nurses intervened. My father wished to profit from his enforced inactivity, and took the opportunity to transcribe his knowledge of music. It gave me great pleasure to collaborate with him.

The atmosphere I had known in the hospitals in Istanbul and that of the London hospitals were quite different. Here, there was little contact between patients. No one wished to speak about the cause of their pain, as if they wished to hide it. In contrast to the Istanbul hospitals, which seemed to hold more visitors than patients, my impression was that here few people came to visit their sick friends or relations. As for us, although we were foreigners, on weekends we had a large number of visitors. It was during one such visit that a group from Colet House asked my father's approval for me to instruct them in the playing of ceremonial music. So, on Tuesdays, I went to teach the little that I knew of the music of *sama'* to about thirty members of the Colet House group, who were highly motivated and were all much older than me. I believe the saying to be true that the best way to learn for oneself is to try to teach others. The results were not without success, and some weeks later I began to direct the ceremonial music.

What with these classes and the people I had met on my previous visit to England, I found myself surrounded by friends. Robert and I often went to visit Miss Rina, an old lady who, with her white hair and piercing blue eyes, was always seated on her rocking chair and surrounded by her cats, and gave the impression of coming straight out of an Agatha Christie novel. As she stayed up late almost every night, her door was always open to a circle of friends who came to see her into the small hours. I often came with my *ney*, to which she listened with eyes closed, even forgetting the glass of whisky she held in her hand. Each week her adopted daughter Yvonne brought us food, which Miss Rina had prepared for my father. As she was the head cook at a big London hotel, we always looked forward to Yvonne's arrival – especially me because, like all young men, I had a ferocious appetite, and would often eat hard-boiled eggs to keep from being hungry during the day.

During my stay in London, which lasted nearly six months, my father's state of health deteriorated so much that I had to help him with the most basic needs. One evening he looked at me and said, 'You know, I am thinking of a story', and then told me the following:

In a village there was a man who lived with his son, wife and father, the latter old and both physically and mentally very weak. The wife, who did not like the presence of the old man in the house, was always urging her husband to get rid of his father. The old man became the subject of frequent quarrels between the couple. The young man resisted his wife's injunctions until one day, in a fury, she gave him an ultimatum: 'It is him or me – if your father is not out of the house by tomorrow, I will be the one who leaves.'

The young husband, in a quandary, finally gave into his wife's demand. The next day, early in the morning, he helped his father into a small cart and told him that they were going to the mountain with his grandson. After a long and sad journey, they finally arrived at the top. He carried his father out of the cart, settled him as best he could and told him that he was going to look for something with his son and that they would be back later. So, they set out on the long return journey. As it was getting dark, the child asked his father, 'Are we not going back to fetch my grandfather?'

The father, ill at ease, answered, 'From now on, your grandfather will stay there. He will not be coming home anymore.'

'How is that possible?' asked the child.

The father answered, 'You see, my son, when parents become too old, one takes them to the mountain and leaves them there.' The child began to cry; the father stopped the cart and asked his son, 'Are you crying because you love your grandfather so much?'

To which the child answered, 'No I am not crying because of my grandfather, but I am crying for you, because I am thinking of the day when you yourself will have reached the age when I will have to take you to the mountain.' On hearing that, the man turned around, went back to his father and found him in the same place where he had abandoned him. His eyes full of tears, he asked to be forgiven, and was most surprised to see that the old man had just quietly been waiting for him. Asked why he had not felt anxious, the old man replied,

'I myself did not abandon my own father on the mountain so that you in turn, would not abandon me.'

This story, one amongst many my father told to me, left its mark on me to this day. I believe in the reality of the transmission through the generations of good and evil.

After some months had passed, the doctors gave me to understand that the radiation treatment had not produced the anticipated results. In addition, it had become necessary to operate on my father, as the tumour had grown and was beginning to affect his breathing. Obviously, I could not give this bad news either to my father or to my family. We decided to return to Turkey, where we were greeted by a gathering of as many friends as had seen us off. Both of us were convinced that the time passed in London had been more fruitful on a personal level than it had been on a medical one. Finally, when we got back, there was a lot of money left. My father, most fortunately, had not died, so we did not have the expense of returning his coffin to Istanbul.

During all this time I had, of course, missed a lot of school. My lack of qualifications always preoccupied my father, since in Turkey as everywhere else there is little possible future without diplomas. Thus I decided, in order to satisfy him, to try my luck and sit for the university degree entrance examination. It really was a question of luck, as I had no idea of the academic programme necessary to study and pass the exam. I had returned from London at the beginning of May; the exam took place in June. I got in touch with some of my old friends and asked if I could join them in their study preparations. They accepted with good grace.

Miraculously, or lucky as the result of my good intentions towards my father, I succeeded not only in passing the exam but also in entering university. I found myself well-placed in the faculty of economic science. The subject did not interest me in any way, although it was much sought-after by many students. At that time, it was not possible to choose one's own university course, as this was decided by the results of the entrance examination. This was undoubtedly one of my father's last joys. In spite of his illness, he was still working at Broadcasting House and, again, I was lucky: a place became vacant there, and I became part of the orchestra as a *ney* player.

Of all my Turkish friends, Nezih Uzel was and is, without doubt the nearest to me, united as we are by our memories of childhood and our collaboration in musical events. Nezih was a young schoolboy when he first met the *sheik* of the Uzbek *tekke*. While he studied at the French *lycée* at Galatasaray, where young people were brought up with a European cultural outlook with a view to their becoming diplomats or taking part in government, this boy was struck by the Mevlevi tradition and its music. He told his teacher of his interest in Rumi, and was advised to go to Konya. Taking advantage of the winter holiday he went there, and met my father as well as the *sheik* of the Uzbek *tekke*. His life was transformed; he became the favourite disciple of Sheik Necmeddin, and went to live near him.

Having a perfect knowledge of French, he established a bond with a small group of Parisians who had discovered Istanbul and its inhabitants just at the time when the last fires of an authentic tradition were still burning. Hervé Baley and his associates Daniel Ginat and Patrice Goulet, as well as his young brother Pierre-Marie, formed the nucleus. From 1966, their regular visits to Konya and Istanbul gave hope to the Sufi community, which on the whole lacked recognition. The fact that people came from so far away to meet with them at regular intervals was a favourable and encouraging sign.

After the events of May 1968 in Paris, the circle of our French friends inspired by Hervé and his friends, was enlarged. With them, a young man whose Christian name was Olivier (and whom we called in Turkish *Zeytin*, or 'Olive') was the only foreigner who lived in the heart of the community itself. Olivier came from a family in Rheims, and his attitude to life was that of a young man of the 1968 generation – one of revolt against an establishment based on and carrying middle-class values. Beyond this he pursued other ideals, which he hoped to find in the Uzbek *tekke*. He was reserved, even withdrawn; it was rare to catch him smiling, but one felt that 'his head was bubbling over'. He liked to take part in the life of the community, working as one of them, picking over the rice or preparing the *nargile*. He lived with us for almost a year, and then returned to France; we hoped he would return to Turkey for good, as Sheik Necmeddin wished him to, but learned some time later of his death in a motor accident. This loss saddened us all very much.

The first journey to Paris in 1968 (in which I did not take part because of my studies), as well as the second one in 1970, had consolidated ties with our French friends. One day, during the course of that year in Istanbul, my father called me into his office. He had with him a man who could not speak a word of Turkish, and could not make himself understood. It was Deben Bhattacharya, a musicologist originally from Calcutta who was now established in Europe and trying to make links between Eastern and Western music. He was in Turkey with the aim of forming a traditional music ensemble that would perform at the Rikskonserter, a Swedish institute. He had come to seek advice from my father yet, he later confided in me, was so overwhelmed by him that he had spent the whole day by his side and had forgotten the real reason for his visit. Since my knowledge of English had been improved by my stay in London, I acted as translator.

During that day, the idea came to him to include me in the ensemble. This was the start of my personal adventures in Europe. Forty concerts were planned for a tour of several Swedish towns. The context was academic rather than mystical-religious, as I had experienced with the whirling dervishes in France, England and the US. The focus was primarily on the music, which was welcomed and appreciated by the young academics more for its form than for its religious aspect. I found in Sweden a country less enthusiastic towards Sufism than those I already knew. Nevertheless, it was a very pleasant trip. At the end of this tour I had in my possession an air ticket that obliged me to stop either in Paris or Rome. I opted for Paris; this short stay, beginning one day in April 1973, has lasted until today.

On my arrival I was welcomed by Pierre-Marie Goulet, who had for a long time suggested that I come to Paris to continue my studies. Amongst all my European acquaintances, he was the only one who was about my age, and this helped to bring us close together. He had just moved into a studio near the Porte d'Orléans with Posie, a young English girl. He very kindly offered me the possibility of staying with them. His house had been all fitted out in wood, in a somewhat disconcerting style, by his brother Patrice and by his friend Hervé Baley, who were architects of the Frank Lloyd Wright school. They had succeeded in giving a most original style to this place, which was in the backyard of a block of flats. The only drawback was that the whole front was made of glass and directly faced the wall of this apartment block. Pierre-Marie was a little like his house, a flower surrounded by buildings. I thought I understood that his travels in Turkey had greatly contributed to his opening up. Perhaps having me in the house was for him a chance to prolong the rich moments he had known in Istanbul.

Constantinople   Derviches tourneurs

heik Ataullah (centre) and the dervishes of the *tekke* of Pera In Istanbul, *circa* 1910–17.

84. ALEP — Derviches

Dervishes from the *tekke* of Halep, representing the last generation before the restrictions imposed on Sufis and religion in general) following the establishment of the independent Turkish Republic in 1947.

Musicians in the *selamlik* (meeting room) of the Uzbek *tekke* in 1957. From left: Vehbi Durruoglu, Niyazi Sayin, Yekta Akinci, Halil Can, Nafiz Uncu, Cahid Gozkan, Kutahyali Arif and Ekrem Hur.

The Uzbek *tekke* in 1987, halfway through restoration. The *selamlik* had been restored, though not the dining room and the *sheik's* private quarters. The *tekke* has since been completely restored.

My father Ulvi (centre) in the studio of Istanbul's Broadcast House, with Aka Gündüz Kutbay (left) and Hasan Dede (right), in 1966.

Playing the *ney* with my father, 1968. This photo accompanied a newspaper article about my first solo performance, which was broadcast on radio.

The first students of Ahmet Bîcan Kasaboğlu, dancing the *sema* in 1968.

A 1959 meeting of the Uzbek *tekke*. Standing, from left: Gufan (grandson of Sheik Necmeddin), Madame Kudret (the *sheik's* wife), my mother Suheyla Erguner, my father Ulvi Erguner, Sadik (the *sheik's* older brother), my older brother Hulki Erguner, Ethem (the *sheik's* younger son). Seated, from left: Sevket (the *tekke's* cook), Ayse (the *sheik's* granddaughter), Sheik Necmeddin Ozbek Kangay, my younger brother Suleyman and me.

Sheik Muzaffer (left), me and the *sheik's* disciples Tugrul Inançer (also his successor) and Sefer Dal (the *sheik's* first successor), during their visit to France in 1976.

A stop in the former Yugoslavia on the way to Paris, 1970. Standing, from left: Cinuçen Tanrikorur (*oud* player) Ulvi Erguner, Saadeddin Heper (music master of the *tekke* of Pera in Istanbul), Aka Gündüz Kutbay (*ney* player) Selman Tuzun (master of the ceremony), Ahmet Bîcan Kasaboğlu (master of dance). Seated, from left: me (*ney* player), Ziya Akyigit (singer), Dogan Ergin (*ney* player).

Nezih Uzel (left) and me, at London's Almeida Theatre, 1977.

In Pakistan at the home of the great *qawwali* singer Nusrat Fateh Ali Khan (left), with friend (centre), in 1984.

The Erguner Ensemble, 1998. Seated, from left: Necip Gulses (*tanbur*), me (*ney*), Hakan Gungor (*qanun*); standing, from left: Derya Turkan (*kemençe*), Mehmet Emin Bitmez (*oud*).

Playing with my son Selman, 1993.

A few days were enough for me to realise that his generosity and friendship towards me were those of a brother. As for me, after my London experience, I had learned to live in other people's homes as discreetly as possible. Pierre-Marie and Posie liked entertaining. Painters, writers, architects and musicians were always at their table. As I had not yet mastered the language, their discussions over bottles of wine seemed never-ending. 'You have not understood a thing!' was their most frequently used phrase. It was enough for someone to give his opinion on a book or a film for the opposite view to appear. From opinions for, to opinions against, the noise rapidly increased. (These quibbles, which never seemed to come to an end, appeared absurd to me, since in Turkey I had been taught that a man is more important than his work. Thus a work can seem true, but it is nothing if it is made by a false person.) I was living surrounded by these artists, who often showed interest in Sufism. This led me, insofar as my French permitted, to sometimes take part in the conversations.

Pierre-Marie and Hervé organised my admission into the special school of architecture in the Boulevard Raspail. A bit like a leaf in the wind, I followed my destiny. My confidence in my ability was often swept by anxiety. It seemed impossible to follow studies in French while my fluency in this language left much to be desired. Furthermore, I did not have the means to stay in France for long while studying at a private school. All I had in my pocket was what was left of the money from the Swedish tour, but I still had my open ticket (valid for one year) to return to Istanbul, just in case.

Nevertheless, I tried. I signed up at the Alliance Française to learn French but, as this turned out to be quite expensive, I could only stay there for a month. My solution to this was to buy a small dictionary and choose fifty words each day to memorise while walking around the Parc Montsouri near where I lived. Certainly the people who saw me each day strolling about while endlessly repeating odd words must have taken me for a loony, but it was the only way I found to learn the language.

At the beginning of the winter, I started my studies in architecture. The other students could not understand how someone who spoke so little French could have been admitted to the university. I tried, against all odds, to hold on tight. I still remember the first day when a stream of motorbikes rushed in front of the school with a thundering noise. The free behaviour of the young students was shocking to me. They could go into a classroom with a bottle of beer, answer back to a teacher or leave the room in the middle of a lecture. In Turkey, any of this would have been unthinkable. Some of them explained to me that this was the outcome of May '68. Architecture was the main subject of exchanges; one could feel that they had all dreamed of learning this profession. The strong motivation of the French students was very different from that of the Turkish students, whose university entrance is compulsory according to their results in a competitive examination. This is why many students in Turkey are only vaguely interested in the subject of their courses. The French are truly privileged! Student life in Paris was also very pleasant. Unlike in London, it did not take long for me to feel at home. I discovered the city, its monuments and its cafés, during long walks in my fellow students' company.

Although I was introduced somewhat by chance to the world of architecture, I was becoming passionately interested in the subject. Unfortunately, I began to feel the harsh reality of my financial situation. I was always sure that one's subsistence came from God, and that He was able to create the most unimaginable conditions to provide for it. Alas, human doubt is stronger than certainty. At the end of the year, I decided to say my farewells to all and return to Turkey. In Istanbul, I registered at the School of Economics. Also, during the summer, just as the doctors had warned us, my father's health had worsened. Now, every day, he was spitting out bits of his lungs. He was very weak. Because of his disease, he had lost part of his face and could only communicate by writing a few words on bits of paper.

My father thought, and rightly so, that my return to Turkey was due to my worry for him. He encouraged me to go back to Paris, where he was convinced I should continue to find my way. Foreseeing financial problems, he proposed to help me by selling some of his possessions. As I did not want to put my parents in a difficult situation, I lied to them and told them I had everything I needed.

On the 7th of November 1974, I decided to go back to Paris. I took the plane, with two *francs* in my pocket, after what was to be my last farewell to my father. On arrival, I hoped to find Pierre-Marie waiting for me at the airport, but there was no one there. While I was in Turkey, he had sold his house in the Porte d'Orléans and gone to live with his wife in the little village of Desmont, near Pithiviers. It was a large farmhouse in the middle of a field of beetroots. He offered me his hospitality. It was a real joy for me to live again with my Parisian family, and with the children who called me 'Uncle Koukou'.

As I no longer had the means to live in Paris, I had no other choice but to accept. So I found myself in this farm, which consisted of two buildings. Pierre-Marie and his family lived in the one, which had already been converted. The other was not yet renovated; they offered me part of this building and, after having cleaned up and dealt with the mice, I settled in. The comfort was most rudimentary: there were no lavatories, no shower, not even running water. They lent me an oil-fired stove, but it had the unpleasant habit of exploding in the middle of the night, leaving me covered in black soot.

Fortunately, I had the few books which I had brought with me. I started a life of retreat. Paris was too far to enable me to travel there every day to pursue my studies and improve my knowledge of French. Strangely enough, I was not worried about the future – quite the opposite. I felt a certain pleasure in this solitary life, which was eased by the enjoyable presence of the Goulet family. My life was filled with reading and personal research. In this small village, where nobody either spoke or greeted one another, I felt a little like Dervish Tufan of the Uzbek *tekke*.

During this time, my contacts with Istanbul were essentially through the exchange of letters. To telephone, then, took so long, and was so complicated, that I preferred to write. I received a letter once a week from my mother, who gave me news of my father and tried to give me moral support.

And yet it was not through her that I learned the sad news of my father's death. He had died just one week after my departure from Istanbul, at the time I began to live in Desmont. In order not to sadden me, and above all to avoid my hurried return, my mother did not tell me. I heard that my father had died from a Turkish friend who had come back from Istanbul and had himself read about it in a newspaper. Even though my father's long illness had prepared me for the fatal outcome, this definitive separation was very painful.

This secluded country life went on. Pierre-Marie lent me an old *deux chevaux*, but I hardly had the means to put petrol in it. The rare times I went to Paris I could not stay there, as I had no lodgings. Materially, it was one of my most difficult times.

In one of her letters my mother, whom I kept in the dark about my financial difficulties, asked me to get her a pressure-cooker, a special pot she had been dreaming about for a long time. I immediately enquired about the price, which at that time was as much as 110 *francs*. The bank account that I had opened during my first stay in France was in dreadful straits. I had 600 *francs* at the most. I really had to keep aside the sum of 450 *francs*, which was the price of a student plane ticket to Istanbul, so I was hardly in a position to spend more than 150 *francs*. But I had to buy this pressure-cooker, and did buy it, reducing to nothing the money I could spend apart from the cost of my air ticket. I left the pressure-cooker at Patrice Goulet's house for him to keep until my return to Istanbul.

A few days later something amazing happened. When in Paris, I used to stay with Patrice. It was there that I was contacted by a Madame Jeanne de

Salzmann, whom I later learned was at the head of the Gurdjieff movement. She explained to me on the telephone that at the beginning of the century she had lived in Istanbul, very close to the *tekke* of Pera. As it was still functioning at that time, she had been present at several ceremonies which took place there. She had learned that I played the *ney*, and wanted to introduce me to a few of her friends one evening, during which she proposed that I play. I accepted this invitation with pleasure, very happy to be able to meet people interested in the *ney*.

The day of the invitation arrived. The Gurdjieff Institute was near Porte Maillot. That evening, many personalities involved in the Gurdjieff movement were assembled, for whom I played some *taksim* (improvised music) before a Turkish meal was served. At the end of the evening Madame de Salzmann discreetly gave me an envelope and, looking at me straight in the eyes, said, 'With this you will buy a present for your mother.' I took the envelope, thanking her. That evening when I opened it, I found a 500-*franc* note. For me, that was the sign of a real miracle.

Within the next two days I received a call from Bernard Mauguin, a producer at Radio-France and a specialist in Turkish music, whom I had met during that evening. He made me an offer to accompany him in his programmes for France Musique. This was the beginning of my life as a professional musician. Today I can say that everything I have been able to earn playing music started with this pressure-cooker.

We made a series of programmes for France Musique; then the record label Ocora proposed that I record an album. Just as this offer had been made to me, my friend Nezih Uzel came to Paris, accompanied by Saadedin Heper, to lead a workshop organised by a group of Jungian psychologists.

With Nezih I was invited to play in Deben Bhattacharya's home. I accompanied Nezih on my *ney* while he sang *ilahi* (hymns), accompanying himself on his *bendir* (a frame drum). Deben recorded the event. The first album of Sufi music published by Ocora was made from this recording. Soon afterwards, Bernard Mauguin recorded me at the Gurdjieff centre in Paris, and published an album in the UNESCO collection 'Musical Sources' under the title *Meditations on the Ney*.

The publications of these two albums created problems for me. I was, in effect, officially still a student, and as such I had to present myself once a year to the Turkish consulate in order to renew my passport. For this it was necessary to obtain a letter from the cultural attaché certifying that I really was a student. Very proud of having made a record, I wanted to offer him one. That was a mistake. When he saw the record sleeve, he flew into a rage. For him it was unthinkable, and even scandalous, that a young man studying in Paris could be preoccupied with such 'old-fashioned' music. He took out from a cupboard a record made in Berlin by a contemporary Turkish orchestra, in the style of European symphonic music, and thrust it under my nose. It was the work of five Turkish composers commissioned by the government. This type of music, without doubt, conformed more to what he supposed should represent a music worthy of a 'modern' state.

The same misadventure happened with an album recorded in the UNESCO collection *Anthology of the Musics of the World – Turkey* in two volumes, published under the direction of my father. Jacques Bornoff, international adviser for music at UNESCO, recounted to me that in his time he had received a visit from Nevit Kodalli, a great composer and also president of the Turkish committee of UNESCO. The latter had strongly protested against the publication of these two volumes, emphasising the backward and outdated character of the music it contained. For *Meditations on the Ney*, which I had composed and performed, Mr Bornoff had probably received similar objections. I had forgotten to what extent traditional music could unleash the systematic opposition of the Turkish authorities.

These two albums established my name and gave me the the opportunity to play in several small concerts. Nezih and I undertook a series of recitals, or rather workshops, at which people interested in Sufi music or in traditional Turkish music would gather. At the end of these workshops we had exchanges, during which we tried to answer in a Sufi manner the many questions which were asked. In this way, we tried to bring back the old tradition of *sohbet* such as we had known in our youth. This tradition, contrary to how it is generally thought of in Europe, did not have an intellectual character, but related to the present moment. It took the form of short subjective sentences, which sometimes had double meanings and evoked thoughts of a spiritual nature. It was a spontaneous invitation to awakening, and a way of enabling knowledgeable men to express themselves. For me, it was a real pleasure to find a link again with the *sohbet* within a context of our choice. These 'Sufi concert-workshops' were rather successful, even abroad. Working in this way we were invited to perform in small theatres in Italy, Switzerland, the Netherlands and England.

Apart from being interesting meetings they were a source of financial support, which was not an insignificant thing considering my difficulties in this area. I must admit that quite often I had to sleep on a bench in a Parisian park; these small fees were not sufficient to allow me to rent a room, even a modest one.

Fortunately, at that time, a very warm relationship began with Madame de Salzmann. She would invite me to her large flat in the Sixteenth Arrondissement and would share with me her memories of her journeys in Turkey with Gurdjieff. She recounted how, together, they had been to many *sama'* in the *tekke* of Istanbul. Her memories could just as well have been those of a member of our community. I listened to this elderly lady, enchanted. It was wonderful, in the heart of Paris, to be able to hear a side of Istanbul evoked which I knew so well! In spite of the great difference in our ages, I felt very close to Madame de Salzmann, a lady with a remarkable mind who succeeded in bringing together great respect, great authority and an uncommon sense of humour.

One day, she asked me where I lived. I told her that friends put me up here and there, but that I had no proper lodgings. She then proposed to help me, with the assistance of Elisabeth Bombright, who was a trustee of an American foundation. This foundation gave me a small grant and, in return, I was to write a document on Sufi music. It was a small grant, but enough to convince a landlord to rent me a small studio.

At last, I could have a space of my own! It was a small room in the servants' quarters on the ninth floor of a building in Rue Saint-André-des-Arts. Comfort was minimal. Electricity was provided through a makeshift connection to the floor below (a simple radiator blew the fuse). It was so damp that I could never sleep in the bed, but only sitting, as best I could, on a stool. Still, it was warmer than outside. Although I am not very tall, the only place I could stand up in the room was near the door. This cubby-hole had no toilet (I had to go down three flights of stairs to find one), and no shower. There was just a tiny washbasin with no hot water, so I had to call on sympathetic friends to be able to wash myself. But anyway, I had a roof over my head!

Soon after my arrival at Rue Saint-André-des-Arts, I found I had to help a fellow citizen, a philosophy student with a grant from the Turkish government. I had met him at the Paris Mosque, a place that inspired me less for the Friday prayers than for the small community of fellow students whom I met there. One day, he sent a message asking to see me urgently. I went right away to his small flat in the Pantin district where he lived with his wife and two children. I found his wife in tears. Deeply depressed, he had tried to commit suicide. The owner of the flat had called an ambulance, and he was going to be taken into hospital, but his wife was totally against this. In the midst of the overall turmoil, I took it upon myself to tell the doctors that my friends were leaving for Turkey the next day. I succeeded in convincing them not to insist. To send him back to Turkey was, no doubt, the right solution. Unfortunately, the family had no money; I had to pay for all the expenses of the journey. The whole of my American grant was spent on the purchase of the tickets. Once more, I found myself penniless and with rent to pay. (This friend is, today, an eminent philosophy professor at the University of Istanbul.)

This 'good deed', however, brought me luck. A few days after my friend's departure, Nezih and I were invited by Mrs Carlways, who was in Paris at the time, to the house of Peter Ustinov's ex-wife, who lived in a large apartment near the Elysée. During the evening they asked Nezih to sing and me to accompany him on the *ney*. We were happy to do this. That evening, Françoise Gründ, the wife of Sherif Khaznadar, was present. (Together they directed the Festival of Traditional Art in Rennes.) They both became great friends of mine, sharing my passion for the traditional music of the world. Thanks to them, I took part in the Rennes festival several times. Later on, I undertook many other projects with them, with great pleasure.

NINE

Classical Music from Turkey and the Western Audience

The first concerts of traditional Turkish music in Europe took place in the Seventies. France, following the events of 1968, seemed to me to experience a period when intellectual curiosity was flowering, together with a respect for and lively interest in cultures outside Europe. If we in the East used to see universality in Western culture, I soon realised that in Europe there was a less ethnocentric view than it seemed at first sight. The wave of interest in Sufism at the time made me aware that this universality was not all 'Eurocentric' but included a more global vision, aiming to give greater value to the expressions of cultures from all over the world.

Through the Sufi concerts given with Nezih, I found that I was one of the pioneers of the introduction in Europe of a whole new wave of traditional arts, which were being discovered by an enthusiastic public. Numerous personalities from the world of arts and culture contributed strongly, and still do, to make these 'non-European' cultures known. Sherif Khaznadar and Françoise Gründ in France; Laurent Aubert (founder of the Ateliers d'Ethnomusicologie in Geneva) in Switzerland; Habib Touma (responsible for the Music Institute of Berlin) in Germany; Pierre Audi (director of the Almeida Theatre in London) in the UK; Marie Carmen Palma (former director of the Granada Festival) in Spain; Tineke de Jonge (founder of the RASA cultural centre in Utrecht) in the Netherlands; and Franco Laera (who ran an experimental theatre in Italy), as well as a number of other people, all played a mediating role between a public avid for new discoveries and the artists who found opportunities through them to present their musical heritage. Later on, these connections allowed me to introduce some musician friends, whirling dervishes and musicians coming either from the classical or the popular Turkish traditions, whom I helped to profit from this European fascination with non-European music.

With increasing numbers in the audience, the concerts could obviously not remain on the scale of these small workshops of Sufi music, which I had directed here and there with Nezih in Europe. From then on it was necessary to develop what was presented onstage, and for something more substantial to be seen and heard. With this in mind, I invited the whirling dervishes of Istanbul.

From the Eighties, certain figures from the performing arts – Thomas Erdos, for example, a prolific artistic advisor to performance festivals around the world – joined us to organise several tours for the whirling dervishes. We were departing from the narrow circle of people interested in mysticism that I had known in the Seventies, and were entering a more general cultural *milieu*. The audience was now interested in the dance as much as in the music, and no longer only in the religious and mystical aspects of the performances.

During a ceremony that we presented at the Théâtre du Rond-Point des Champs-Elysées, I had a very amusing adventure. At the end of the performance, I was surrounded by a great number of acquaintances and Turkish friends who had just taken part in the ceremony. As is the custom, verses from the Qur'an had been recited at the end. Suddenly, I felt a hand on my left shoulder. Turning around, I saw Eva de Vitray-Meyerovitch, the well-known translator of Rumi's works, accompanied by friends of hers interested in Islam. She asked me what the numbers were of the Qur'anic verses that had just been recited. At the same moment, someone tapped me on my right shoulder. It was the hand of the man who had recited the Qur'an, and he wanted to know how much a drink at the Moulin Rouge would cost, as he wanted to go there with friends. In the confusion of the moment, I mixed up replies. I gave the price of a glass of whisky at the Moulin Rouge to Eva de Vitray-Meyerovitch and the number of the verses of the Qur'an to the reciter!

One day, we were invited to the Temple of Great Orient by some Freemason friends who told us, quite rightly, that as we performed ceremonies in churches, there was no reason not to do the same in their temple. For us, to present a Sufi ceremony in a Freemason temple was not obvious, because, in Turkey, Freemasonry has political connotations. We accepted, however, on condition that the doors be open to an uninitiated public. On the day, we were shown into a little room to prepare ourselves for the ceremony. I was greatly embarrassed when I noticed that one of the members of our community had got hold of the symbolic hammer, which belonged to the master of the lodge, to tap in a nail that was sticking out of the sole of his shoe! Our Freemason friend who had arranged this presentation did not know how to behave in front of such a blunder. Finally, everything was sorted out, and the hammer was presented as a gift to the man who had turned cobbler on that occasion.

At the end of the ceremony, there was a discussion between Freemasons and Sufis about their respective symbols and ideas. We were quite used to this kind of exercise, and willingly participated. One of the Freemasons asked to be given an explanation of the symbolism of the triangle, which had been traced by the Sufi master at the beginning of the ceremony. I did not see very well what this person was alluding to, but I put the question to the one who had taken on the role of the master. He answered simply that, just before sitting down, he had noticed three little bits of paper lying on the floor which by chance formed a triangle. To pick them up more easily, he had licked the tips of his fingers. This had been taken by our Freemason friends as a most significant mystical, symbolic gesture. They would not believe in the simplicity of this explanation. They even congratulated us for our way of resisting the temptation of revealing our 'secrets'.

As all these ceremonies were very well received in Europe, I thought I would use this fact to weaken the Turkish authorities' negativity towards Sufism in general, and towards the whirling dervishes in particular. I argued that this 700-year-old tradition aroused the interest of the whole world, and that, consequently, it would be a great pity to let it die out in the very country where it had such considerable importance. I suggested that one of the *tekke* that had been relegated to a museum should be brought back to life, but my efforts were in vain. However, the success of the whirling dervish ceremonies in Europe gave birth, in Istanbul, to a multitude of small groups which called themselves 'whirling dervishes'. Turkish travel agencies, which had begun to include performances of dervishes in their programmes, certainly had something to do with this development. This is a clear example of the perverse effects of organised tourism. From these events, tourism was no longer at the service of culture, but culture had become a tool for tourism.

As we were reaching a larger European audience (and no longer one only directed towards mysticism), our approach was becoming rather ambiguous, somewhere between a performance and an authentic religious ceremony. This duality obliged us to make a choice.

Traditionally, as the ceremony was not considered to be a dance, no specific costume was demanded of the participants. What counted above all was what each one was experiencing in the depth of his being. Furthermore, musical skill was not the most important thing. In this respect, I remember having participated in ceremonies, both in Konya and in Istanbul, where the instruments were badly tuned and the singers out of time with the music, yet the right feeling and the truth of the ceremony could be experienced.

With European audiences, we made it a point of honour to perform the ceremony with perfect technique. The dancers had to be exact in their gestures while they whirled at great speed, and the musicians precise in their execution. While the ceremony benefited from these improvements, it lost the undefinable touch which gave it its real authenticity. One can easily realise the difference when comparing recordings from the archives of that epoch with those made nowadays. As a musician who has known the two forms of expression, I am convinced that it is possible to bring together precision, technique and right feeling. In fact, it is probably the only way to revitalise this form, which is at the same time artistic and spiritual.

With all these concerts of traditional music, and with the ceremonies of the whirling dervishes, our relationship with the public was becoming very strange. Until then, Orientalists and ethno-musicologists had played the role of intermediaries between European and non-European cultures. In inviting, as I did, artists from distant horizons to meet the European public, the cultures were brought together. A certain conflict developed. To begin with, the musicologists saw my musical activities as illustrating their concepts. The more I took on a European way of life, the more I was in a position to express the substance of my own tradition. Without being in open warfare, I was, however, the object of some criticism. Some musicologists reproached me for being too much at the forefront with concerts and recordings, and for wanting to give my own interpretation of my musical tradition. Not only did it seem to them that I was encroaching on their field of knowledge, but that I was also the instigator of a popularisation they abhorred on principle.

Relations with the Orientalists who worked on Sufism and Rumi were better, inasmuch as the performances of the ceremonies served to promote the works they published on the subject. Very often our tours were preceded by newspaper articles written by these learned people. Even though we were not always in accordance with what they put forward, it was very difficult to prove them wrong. They often had a propensity towards the symbolic aspect of the ceremony. For example, for them the headdress of the dervish was meant to symbolise a tombstone, and his white robe a shroud, with these attributes signifying awareness of death. They saw that the dervish, when he whirls, turns his right hand towards the sky, while the left is bent towards the earth. Some Orientalists seemed to consider the dervish as a sort of lightning conductor connecting Heaven and Earth. Certainly, if one studies the ancient texts, 'poetic images' can be found which express this meaning, but they have nothing to do with symbolism. They are simply poetic interpretations which are neither explanations nor definitions. The public was thus diverted from the fundamental meaning of the whirling dervishes ceremony, which is that it is, above all, a contemplative religious ceremony which brings about a specific ecstatic state.

I can remember a meeting at the Abbey of Senanque where a large number of Jungians were present. Their questions covered techniques and other details of Sufism. Someone asked what the rhythmical formula was that was used in the ceremonies. I answered that, in fact, at one point in the ceremony there was a rhythmic cycle of fifty-eight beats. Immediately, one of their members stood up and launched into an incoherent speculation about the symbolism of that number. He insisted that five plus eight equalled thirteen; the one represented Unity, and the three, the Trinity. He developed this explanation until I interrupted him to tell him that I had made a mistake, and the cycle was not fifty-eight but fifty-six beats. He was not put off, however, and reconstructed a whole theory from the latest numbers: five plus six being eleven, one and one representing Unity doubled! If it appeared absurd to us, for them it held great significance.

Generally, this kind of 'observation' was unavoidable. Many misunderstandings arose in our relationships with those who wished to know more about Sufism, originating in the gap between what we were trying to convey of our tradition and what was seen in reality.

One day, I was invited by the writer and journalist Michel Random to the launch of his book *Sufism and Dance*. I was expected to play the *ney* during the reception he gave for the occasion. There were many guests and, when I sat down to play, I was squeezed between several people. As I was playing my *ney*, I was disturbed by a drop of water that fell onto my hand. I took advantage of a pause in my playing to glance at the person sitting next to me; the 'water' was, in fact, tears that had sprung from his eyes! Indeed, they were so plentiful that they wet his trousers and mine. Touched by his sensitivity to my playing, I tried even harder. Once I had finished playing, I turned to him; I looked right into his eyes and put my hand on his shoulder to apologise for having caused him so much feeling. With bloodshot eyes he said to me, 'I am sorry, it is the cat!' This anecdote, beyond its humourous aspect, reveals the rift and misunderstanding between the two worlds.

The success of the presentation of the whirling dervishes in Europe encouraged other dervish communities outside Turkey to perform abroad. Dervish orders existed in a number of countries that were formerly part of the Ottoman Empire, such as Egypt, Greece and the Balkans; in total, there were 110 communities from Yemen to the Maghreb. Some began to claim the tradition of whirling dervishes for themselves (notably the Syrians of Aleppo and Damascus). Due to the French *qanun* player, Julian Weiss (who became 'Celâleddin Julian Weiss'), there is now a group from Aleppo which performs some dances of the whirling dervishes. They present a programme of traditional classical music or religious repertoire, but they do not perform the proper ceremony. I can remember Alain Crombecq, then director of the Avignon Festival, saying that he preferred the whirling dervishes from Syria because they turned more quickly. This kind of criteria for appreciation seems inappropriate to the tradition, to say the least. As a result the Turkish dervishes, in a spirit of competition, tend to whirl a little faster than they used to.

As for the music itself, the rift was of another kind. Our contact with the public and with the European musical world was increasing; we were moving further away from the purely traditional field, and were now in touch with artists from other cultures who were asking us to participate in some of their projects. As far as I was concerned, I was confronted with a new situation. I had a specific cultural heritage and an instrument, the *ney*, which was particularly well-suited to my tradition. To play another type of music was quite a challenge. However, experimenting with several forms of music gave me the chance to improve my skill as an interpreter. I made the *ney* follow melodic lines in a language which was not its own. I found myself in the situation of a Chinese poet obliged suddenly to express himself in a language other than his own. As a consequence, my capacity to express myself was, for a while, diminished.

My first experience in this new musical approach took place at the Institut de Recherche et de Coordination Acoustique/Musique (IRCAM) in Paris, with one of founder and director Pierre Boulez's assistants, the composer Thomas Koestler, who had just written his *Dialogue*. Some famous musicians, such as the clarinetist Michel Portal, had been approached to perform this highly contemporary work. Each performer was linked to a tape recording which started automatically at the smallest vibration. These recordings consisted of background noises and related to the cultural context of each instrument.

Thus my *ney* was supposed to produce sounds from Arab countries and Michel Portal's clarinet, sounds from great European cities.

It was somewhat difficult for me to find my place in this baffling work. This surprised Thomas Koestler because, he told me, when he was writing my part he had taken his inspiration from one of my recordings. I then realised that someone could listen to my playing in a very different way to that which I had expected. In this instance, what he wanted me to play for him seemed to me quite close to the siren of the fire brigade. The parts assigned to the clarinet and to the cello seemed closer to their proper nature.

At the first concert, I realised that the public could not hear much of the sound of the instruments because the background noise was raised to its maximum. On the other hand, the microphone was placed so near to my mouth that my slightest breath triggered off the recording tape. The fee for this performance was ten times higher than that for the concerts in which I had played previously as an interpreter of traditional music. This last fact was significant to me: what I had been trained for had less value than what I was asked to try in the European music system, even though it did not suit me.

This was the start of a number of experiences. I collaborated in the music for Peter Brook's *Mahabharata*, then on Peter Gabriel's *Passion*, the soundtrack for Martin Scorsese's film *The Last Temptation of Christ*. I met Peter Gabriel, whom I did not know at all, at the presentation of the *Mahabharata* in Glasgow. He invited me to Box, south of London, for a few recording sessions. There I found a dream of a place with several recording studios, one of which was in a converted mill. The water that had driven the mill ran under the studio. It was a wonderful place and, moreover, was full of impressive electronic equipment. I was housed in one of the buildings reserved for visitors, and I had the honour of being the first guest to stay in these sumptuous surroundings. I was also one of the first musicians to participate in Peter's label Real World, a great project that was, I believe, the starting point of the 'world music' movement.

This collaboration was very interesting, as Peter left ample room for improvisation. We spent several hours together, with him singing and accompanying himself on his synthesiser, and me responding on the *ney* to his musical lead. This resulted in a real friendship. I was touched by the gentleness and sensitivity of his music (even though he belongs to the rock music world) and by the great respect and attention he gave to other people's music. I would like to believe that this is not only a result of the legendary good manners of the British.

A less pleasant experience happened with the composer Jean-Michel Jarre.

A friend, who became his adviser in traditional music for Jean-Michel's great project for the bicentennial of the French Revolution, brought him an extract of a recording made at the Abbey of Senanque. Without my knowledge, Jean-Michel wrote a work titled *Revolution*, inspired by one of my improvisations. He had re-used one of my musical motifs, adding rhythm and violins, and had spliced some passages with a synthesiser. The album produced from this work, which I only discovered later, left me quite perplexed. I was puzzled by its musical pertinence and unpleasantly surprised that only the words 'traditional music' appeared on the album cover. I was listed only as interpreter, and not as composer. Was this the European way of seeing things? It seemed that music coming from 'elsewhere' was from the outset considered as traditional and public property. Traditional music, however, could only survive with the presence and the creativity of artists. My improvisations are specifically mine, even though they are based on the modal system called *maqam* (a set of notes with traditions that define relationships between them and their melodic development). I was advised to take legal action, and I won the case easily, having proved that the work was my own composition. My rights as an author were acknowledged; I co-signed the work for the Société des Auteurs, Compositeurs et Editeurs de Musique (SACEM) with Jean-Michel, with whom I am now on good terms. This adventure led me to subsequently take more precautions with any recording I made.

These various collaborations with European musicians enabled me to become recognised not only in Europe but also in my own country. In Turkey, new generations brought up on European culture (which they consider universal) were suddenly confronted with an artist playing a traditional instrument amongst European musicians of international repute. Young people, who had until then refused to listen to this instrument, were at first intrigued and then seduced by the way in which certain Western musicians were using it.

On the other hand, although there had been some well-known musicians, a certain anonymity had hitherto always prevailed in the world of traditional music. Whereas in Europe, the composer's name is always linked to his work – one speaks of the music of Bach, of Mozart, etc. This had never been the case in Turkey, where music has always existed with the composer's name being secondary. The music is differentiated by its richness of melody, and not by its style or the current musical fashion. The contact of Turkish traditional music with Western music brought more importance to the artistic expression of the performer. This is how I became known as the representative of traditional music in Turkey.

This was evident during the first concerts I gave at the International Istanbul Music Festival (IIMF). This event, which was sponsored by a very wealthy man from the pharmaceutical industry, aimed to promote Western culture in Turkey. From this point of view, it seemed incongruous to suddenly include traditional Turkish music. Previously, more or less official groups of this type of music, who came from the music conservatories, were exclusively European-style orchestras, seventy to eighty musicians directed by a conductor. These orchestras attracted only a small audience, not much larger than the number of musicians on the stage. The success of my first involvement in this festival surprised me. The *ney* performance drew a large audience. This proved that traditional music, provided it was authentic and not interpreted in a Western way, could draw a proper audience. Without intending to, I subsequently found myself to be one of the pioneers in the renewal of traditional music. I do not know if this was accidental, or if what was happening to me had a more profound significance.

I was invited for several consecutive years to the IIMF. Regularly revisiting my country for this annual festival gave me the opportunity to meet with a wider circle, far beyond the small Sufi society of my childhood. I was now facing the Turkish audience at large, and what a feeling this gave me! I could not forget that I owed this wider recognition to my European experiences. These new perspectives encouraged me to take on a mission. Of course I had to continue my activities as a musician all over the world but, in Turkey specifically, I wanted to help music lovers to discover some musical themes which until then had not been known due to Turkish political culture. Amongst these projects, I offered the audience the liturgical songs of Istanbul, the city being a real mosaic of religious communities. In so doing, I tried to bring together Armenian, Greek, Jewish and Muslim singers, and to create a dialogue between them and myself, enabling a large audience to discover their own religious musical traditions. Here again, only the authority acquired through my international activities enabled me to realise this project.

I was also involved with traditional singing. In Turkey, as in other Muslim countries, the style had become obsolete. With the advent of the microphone many singers used chest voices, which are more sensitive and moving, while in the past more nasal vocal techniques, like that of the *muezzins* who call the faithful to prayer in Islam, were used. The high-pitched voice was abandoned in classical singing. Some research led me to Yusuf Bilgin, who sang in a mosque. He had little musical knowledge, but was gifted with a splendid and especially powerful voice. Together we worked to rediscover these ancient singing techniques. Little by little I introduced new singers to an educated and Westernised Istanbul society, which until then had disregarded them.

I also organised a women's choir, which performed a work I titled *Harem Music*. It was based on a repertoire composed mostly from the songs of the women of the Ottoman palaces, who led separate lives from men, and whose intimacy gave rise to these songs which accompanied their daily activities. This choral work was a success in Turkey and in Europe. In Europe, the audience believed that this work followed a direct line of a tradition, and was not seen as a rediscovery, a re-creation, after half a century's interruption – as *harems* ceased to exist after the fall of the Ottomans. The European concert-goers did not fully realise that the repertoire no longer had any relation to the lives of women in Turkey today.

I then put together an ensemble to interpret the Greek musical repertoire called *rebetiko*. This repertoire had been taken back to Greece at the beginning of the century by Greek immigrants in Turkey who returned to their country, having been expelled under political circumstances. The repertoire was considered to have been limited to melodies from the Aegean and Izmir regions, and also included popular songs from Istanbul adapted to and sung in Greek. Following my search for old recordings, I discovered and transcribed old 78 RPM records. I used a Turkish interpretation to put together the *rebetiko* group in Istanbul.

All these creations were a kind of applied musicology. I was not only trying to bring to light past repertoires that had been lost, but also to re-interpret them. I found financial and moral support from some private Turkish institutions. Some of these works were presented to European audiences and produced in CD format.

In Turkey, for a large part of the audience and for many artists who followed my lead in this research, traditional music is no longer considered to be derived from one source but rather the synthesis of many streams of different origins: popular, scholarly, religious … The rebirth of this diverse repertoire was in opposition to the homogeneity of traditional music favoured by academic orchestras, who still to this day do not acknowledge the cultural origin of the themes they perform.

I think that, to a large extent, I have won the battle for the recognition and appreciation of traditional music by the Turkish intelligentsia, who until then were only willing to appreciate European culture and music. If, formerly, certain circles listened to traditional music, it was less out of preference than from a show of extreme nationalism, political conviction or social identification. I always refused to accept the support of nationalist and chauvinistic groups, even though they were ready to listen to me sympathetically. I felt their motivation was far from being purely artistic.

The fashion in Europe for 'world music' led a number of traditional musicians to adapt their performances to this new form of expression. Already much traditional music had been reduced to a merely popular role in its country of origin. Indian Muslim *qawwali* music, for example, which was a great success in Europe thanks to the great Pakistani singer Nusrat Fateh Ali Khan, initially derived from a musical and literary art of great refinement. It consisted of a sequence of chants that began with thanks to God, based on poems praising God (*hamd* and *munadjat*). However, when I visited Pakistan, I discovered that this style of music was performed under circumstances other than those for which it had traditionally been intended. It had been adapted for religious or private ceremonies such as marriage or circumcision, and was now an indispensable part of these events. Some ten years before my meeting with Nusrat Fateh Ali Khan, *qawwali* was accompanied by Indian classical instruments. Little by little these were replaced by the portable harmonium, the sound of which unavoidably reminded me of a French *bal musette*. This kind of ambiguity exists in the performance of traditional music all over the world; the changes of function transform the musical form.

In Europe, an attempt had been made to rediscover musical traditions using authentic instruments. These criteria were forgotten with the appearance of 'world music'. Under this influence, the traditional musician began to emphasise virtuosity to obtain a music more flattering and easy to listen to. Doubtless they were now playing lively traditional music: lively because it had attracted a real following in its country of origin. But traditional music was corrupted by conforming to the tastes of a less and less educated audience. Consequently, this phenomenon reinforced the change in the countries from which traditional music originated.

Sometimes I find myself dreaming of a world that is not 'Eurocentric'. Europe, following the Industrial Revolution and colonial conquests, imposed its powerful hegemony in the economic and cultural domain. Imagine the situation reversed, the Middle East dominating the rest of the world. Imagine, then, an ethno-musicologist from Baghdad researching German music. If he wrote that Bach's music belonged to German folklore, would this not appear strange to a European? In the contemporary situation, from a European standpoint, the tendency is to consider Chinese and Indian music as belonging to one and the same world, while in India alone there exist not one but several specific musical traditions: northern or southern music, popular, court and religious music, each one performed in its own context. From a European perspective, they are too easily put together under the category of 'ethnic music', whereas in Germany, France or Italy, alongside popular music, there is scholarly or 'classical music'. In 'world music', the criterion of appreciation is no longer the quality of the context or interpretation, which represents the music's true value, but quantity – the greatest number of countries and cultures that can be included.

I am now facing another challenge. In literature, Shakespeare cannot be reduced to English folklore but has universal value, just as Rumi does not belong either to Turkish or Islamic folklore; his value is also universal. In the same way, some so-called 'traditional', scholarly music from Turkey, India or China has as much value as some so-called 'classical' European music. Turkey inherited a complex and refined music from the height of Ottoman culture. However, the duality between Turkish and European contexts that I continue to experience allows me to avoid misunderstandings as well as the conditioning to which it is so easy to fall victim in an era devoid of culture.

My last participation in the Konya festival took place in 1977. Seeing the decadence of these events, I was convinced that it was necessary to remove the ceremony of the whirling dervishes from the monopoly of the Konya tourist office. In 1981, with the help of a Mr Langlois (the cultural development director at UNESCO), Thomas Erdos, Sherif Khaznadar (now director of the Maison des Cultures du Monde) and Habib Touma, I gathered together the Mevlevi community in Istanbul. My intention was to raise the quality of already-existing forms that had fallen into a pitiful state. In Istanbul there were, in effect, five main Mevlevi centres. In the past, literary and musical culture had flourished in Istanbul. The *tekke* of Pera, which had held one of the highest places in the tradition, needed to be revitalised, and no longer be just a cheap museum.

We found a legal solution by creating an association, The Friends of the Tekke of Pera or The Friends of the Mausoleum of Sheik Galip (his mausoleum is located in the *tekke's* garden). In this way, it became possible to officially bring life back to this site without it appearing to be exclusively a brotherhood. I succeeded in convincing some of my Istanbul friends, including Nezih Uzel, to participate. With the help of all these people, I could put together a group of musicians and dancers from Istanbul. Unfortunately, my dreams no longer corresponded with the current reality in Turkey. Many obstacles crossed our way, notably at the political level. Unluckily, there was a new military *coup*. The director of the Konya tourist office, having learned that we were planning a European tour, took offence and wrote to complain directly to General Kenan Evren (who led the *coup* and became President) and prevent us from leaving. His attempt was in vain – we had already left Turkey.

Our tour lasted fifty days, with forty ceremonies performed in Germany, the Netherlands, England, in all the great European cities. Musicians and dervishes together, we were some forty people in all.

The Friends of the Tekke of Pera, which I had founded to counteract the power of the Konya tourist office over the whirling dervishes, did not work out as I had hoped. It rapidly became an Istanbul tourist attraction. European tour operators who included in their programmes an encounter with the dervishes found it easier and cheaper to organise these meetings in Istanbul rather than in Konya. Although I succeeded in counteracting the prestige attributed to the current 'Konya folklore', I could not stop the tourist office from appropriating the Istanbul *tekke* of Pera. In the end, our experience was reduced to meetings at Nezih's house, where he was teaching the *sama'* to a few young men.

We failed in our project to restore the community. The new generations did not have the same focus of interest as their forefathers. Furthermore, the political and cultural context in Turkey was not favourable to the revival of these traditions, of which we had witnessed the last days. I hope, someday, other flowers might blossom. Nowadays in Turkey there is no respect for the tradition of the whirling dervishes, who are seen only as a folkloric and touristic enterprise. I would have liked to help the Turkish as well as the European intelligentsia to recognise the cultural value of the tradition. This recognition was limited by a false mysticism on the one hand, and a shameless 'folklorisation' on the other. In 1987–8, the Turkish Ministry of Culture decided to create a whirling dervish group within the state department for folklore. It performs nowadays throughout the world, under the name Dervishes of Konya. Outside Turkey, this group is too often considered authentic, while in fact it originated within the ministry.

TEN

Meetings with Peter Brook

In 1975, when I was on holiday in Istanbul, I received a telegram from Madame de Salzmann asking me to welcome one of her friends and to help him during his stay in Istanbul. It concerned the producer and director, Peter Brook, whom I had never heard of at the time. I called him at his hotel and, as I had to go to the Uzbek *tekke* that evening, we arranged a meeting at the landing stage of the ferries which cross the Bosphorus. We did not know each other, so he suggested that he wear a red pullover in order to be recognisable. At the agreed time I went to Karaköy, from where the boats to Üsküdar depart. There I found a gentleman wearing a red pullover accompanied by someone he introduced as his assistant.

Together we made our way to the Uzbek *tekke*, where we had dinner. After that, he expressed a wish to see some of the old districts of Istanbul. I took them both to the old quarter of Samatya and Kum Kapi, where the Patriarch of the Armenian Church resides. We parted after spending a good part of the night strolling about in the ancient streets of the Armenian district. A meeting was agreed for the next day at his hotel.

The following day, I was surprised to find a crowd of journalists and writers (some of whom were well-known) in the hotel lobby, queuing up in the hope of meeting Peter. I had the greatest difficulty making my way towards this figure, whose fame was just beginning to dawn on me. We were able, nonetheless, to meet and proceed with our tour of Istanbul as Madame de Salzmann had wished. For Peter the purpose of this journey was to scout locations for the film *Meetings with Remarkable Men*, in which he was planning to tell the life of Gurdjieff.

On my return to Paris, Madame de Salzmann explained this project to me and asked me to participate as a musician. This essentially involved my collaboration in an important scene at the start of the film, which was both symbolic and magical. It showed a competition between several musicians who must make a mountain resonate through the sole force of their art.

To prepare for the film, we went together to London in order to hear some concerts of traditional music, especially Iranian. Afterwards, I suggested returning to Istanbul with Peter in order to introduce him to some Sufi musicians from my circle. There, I introduced him to Aka Gündüz Kutbay, a friend (albeit my senior) and a well-known player of the *ney*, as well as to two other musicians.

A number of experiments were made for the project. This scene of the competition between musicians led to much questioning. We were highly intrigued; to make a mountain vibrate through music represented an abstraction which was difficult to make our own. Our way of looking at music, each in the style that was familiar to him, did not allow us to imagine that one day we would be able to move mountains. We naïvely swung between stupendous reality and a simple metaphor used by Gurdjieff. Clearly, it involved finding a musical improvisation which would allow the impression of such a phenomenon.

This is how we spent whole days with Madame de Salzmann and several of her group in recording experiments: we, the Turkish musicians, but also Iranian artists like the *zarb* player Djamshid Chemirani or Kiani, the well-known *santur* player. There was also a *tanbur* player, another of the *setar*, an Ashkenazi Jewish singer and an Uzbek man with a very impressive face, who simply sat there.

This period was rich with a number of meetings with members of the Gurdjieff groups. I already knew some, such as Robert Browne and Richard Temple, as well as members of the Paris group. Everyone, beginning with Madame de Salzmann, was very keen for this part of the film to be successful, both cinematographically and on the level of its spiritual significance.

During this period I noticed a surprising difference between the first circle, which was made up of the people near Madame de Salzmann (René Zuber, Henri Tracol, Michel de Salzmann, Jean Sviadok, Pierre Egg and some others who had known Gurdjieff) and the members of the second circle, who had joined the group more recently. While the first, without necessarily being 'wise men', had a kind of 'presence' or aura, and were without pretension, the second had a constrained, not to say 'constipated' attitude. One could sense a kind of fanaticism in their taste for the secrecy with which they surrounded all their activities. The first circle, however, seemed to be free from any inclination towards the occult.

This is probably what happens in any spiritual work. At first, a nucleus is formed around one person from whom emanates light, human warmth, wisdom or truth, be it by their words or actions. From this inner circle that is united round a master, a second one evolves once he or she has disappeared. This is often when an attitude of turning in on oneself occurs as a protection from 'the ordinary' – 'them and us'. At this stage, a cult of memory starts and certain ritual forms appear, all leading to the possibility of sectarianism.

To return to the music, different choices were possible. There were the compositions of Gurdjieff himself, but also those of Thomas de Hartmann, who was one of his pupils. For the film however, we were looking for a different sort of music, and this incurred some difficulty. Madame de Salzmann put forward the Eastern sources of Gurdjieff's compositions. These, coming from a sacred inspiration, had been transcribed so as to be played on a harmonium. De Hartmann later adapted them for the piano. The idea had been to bring to the West a musical idiom that had its source in sacred Eastern tradition.

The music proposed by us Easterners was considered too idiomatic. What was asked of us was to be ourselves, disengaged from our musical and cultural backgrounds. This was not easy to achieve, but inwardly I considered that this was the most interesting approach. It meant breaking with our own backgrounds in order to be in contact with a different truth, and forfeiting the comfort of our own musical languages and cultural heritages. At the time we had a lot of difficulties arriving at something of this kind; there were many attempts! Finally the privilege of 'making the mountain vibrate' fell on my friend Aka Gündüz. Afghanistan was chosen as the 'set' for this part of the film, where we had at the same time to play the roles of actors and musicians.

The shooting of the film started in the spring, at a time of year when the temperature was already high. I was worried, as it was the first time I had travelled further east than my place of birth. I also had the curious sensation of discovering in Afghanistan my own country as it might have been a century earlier. Contacts were easily made, as many Afghans spoke Turkish.

The first takes were shot in the vicinity of Kabul, in a landscape of cliffs and mountains. Thousands of people were gathered there, extras as well as many horsemen, the actors playing Gurdjieff and his father and the group of musicians. It was the first time I witnessed and participated in the making of an important film, and I was most impressed by the means that were brought into play.

For the competition scene, the musicians were to try one after the other to make the mountain resonate in front of an assembly of 'wise men'. In the film, the inhabitants of the surrounding valleys gathered there each year to witness this ritual competition. Peter Brook and Madame de Salzmann had succeeded in finding an extraordinary selection of people to represent the council of wise men. The deep, lined faces of these men were impressive. Afghanistan certainly offers great possibilities for such characterisation: the hard lives of these people, even when they are young, leaves traces on their faces.

Where acting as such was concerned, we the musicians were neophytes, and soon realised the difficulty it represented. Peter would tell us to behave normally, to walk as usual, and it resulted in our walking like sailors off the boat after months of sailing. We became more aware every day of the difficulty of the actor's profession, and yet we had to enter into the role of the characters we were supposed to be. After several attempts, we finally succeeded in doing what Madame de Salzmann and Peter expected from us.

It was amazing to see how Madame de Salzmann, although ninety years old, remained active despite the heat of over 40° Celsius. Standing with an umbrella in her hand to protect her from the sun, she had a presence and liveliness which made everyone admire her. She was like a little girl who realising her dearest wish.

The film's large budget allowed for absurd eccentricities where catering was concerned. The meals, for instance, were made with food brought from England in refrigerated trucks. The musicians, just like the British actors and supposedly for the sake of hygiene, were meant to eat frozen food. Meanwhile, the Afghans were enjoying barbecued dishes of which only the delicious smells could reach us. During the intervals, we could make contact with them. I was surprised by their extreme religious observance, their very great piety. I told one of them, who was of Uzbek origin and spoke Turkish, how surprised I was by such manifestations of devotion, such scrupulous Muslim practice – to which he answered, 'Look, look around you!' As a matter of fact, in this valley, not a single blade of grass was growing. He went on: 'In this void, only the Truth can appear.' He was called 'Aldas' (red stone), and became a good friend of mine.

ELEVEN

Journey in Afghanistan

Once the filming was over, my Turkish friends went back home. As for me, I decided to go visit the birthplace of our Master Celâleddin Rumi, in the north of Afghanistan. The day before leaving, I made an appointment with Aldas at my hotel, to go for a walk with him the next morning. I waited for him until noon; no one came. I came out of the hotel and saw him running towards me. He explained that he had indeed come at the agreed time, but had been forbidden to enter the hotel. In this international establishment, people wearing traditional clothes were not allowed to mix with Europeans. This shocking attitude reminded me of the wish in Turkey to deny at all cost our own cultural identity as we had lived it in the past.

I had asked that my fees for the filming be paid to me in Afghan money, as I meant to remain in the country for a time. So I had a small fortune, which could have allowed me to live comfortably for three or four years in Afghanistan. As it was money that could not be converted into foreign currency, I had proposed to Aldas to give him what was left at the end of my stay. He refused; and yet I knew how poor he was because, one day when we had stayed late during the filming, he was worried about the time the last bus left Kabul to take him to his village. If he missed it, he could not even pay for a shared taxi, although it was very cheap. He persisted in refusing to accept the money I offered him.

I left with Michael Currer-Briggs, Peter Brook's assistant, who was going to the north of the country to scout locations. He drove me up to Mazar-e-Sharif, next to Balkh, the birthplace of Rumi. It was a fantastic journey, during which I had the impression of going back in time. I arrived in Mazar-e-Sharif with very little luggage, dressed as a European, but with the Afghan headdress I had just bought. When I went to the mosque I was not allowed in, as it was thought that – dressed as I was – I could only be a foreigner and therefore, very likely, not a Muslim. But the man who looked after the shoes at the entrance questioned some young Uzbeks who were able to explain and convince him that I was both Turkish and a Muslim. When I came out of the mosque they were waiting for me, happy to meet, for the first time, a Turk from Turkey who had come to visit their town. They took me to a hotel owned by a man named Devlet Han, a Turkoman.

I had just settled in when around twenty *mullahs* came to visit me and to ask many questions about Turkey. They willingly answered my own questions about their country. During this meeting I realised that their looks as well as their mentality had the kind of 'purity' that could be found in Turkey a century ago.

As for me, considering my 'fortune', I could be liberal with my invitations, but this was not possible: as they saw it, there was no question of my paying for anything. Being entertained everywhere, without having to open my purse, I believed I would never be able to get rid of my Afghan fortune before leaving the country.

The first day, feeling tired, I asked permission to retire early. They proposed to come and fetch me the next morning for prayers. I went back to my hotel and to my bed, which was not in a room but in a cubicle with walls which did not reach the ceiling. I soon fell asleep, but was awakened very early in the morning by knocking on the door. Thinking that they were calling me for the morning prayers, I opened the door: there was no one there! I wondered if they were waiting for me downstairs. I made my ablutions and went down. Still no one. I then went to the mosque, thinking I would find my friends there, but apart from some beggars it was quite empty. So I made some *reqats* (prostrations), then returned to my bed. I had just fallen asleep when I was again awakened by knocking on the door. I went back to the mosque again and still saw no one there, made more *reqats*, returned to the hotel and went back to sleep … and so it went, three or four times more. The fourth time, I found someone actually waiting behind the door. I suddenly realised that no one had really knocked at my door. My room was next to the toilets, and the occupants of the other cubicles, when they had to relieve themselves, knocked on the door of the toilets to make sure there was no one inside. This is what made me walk across town to the mosque several times and make a number of *reqats* …

I stayed about ten days in Mazar-e-Sharif and then decided to go to Balkh, which was one or two hours away. I was taken there by my Turkish-speaking Afghan friends. Balkh was one of the great Eastern capitals at the time when Rumi and his father lived there. As I approached I realised that, as I already knew, nothing was left of it apart from the ruins of a mosque and of what must have once been a palace. My thoughts went to the legendary departure of Rumi's father, Bahaeddin Valad, the 'Sultan Ulema' ('*sultan* of the men of knowledge').

At that time, Balkh was governed by Mohamed Harizm Shah, who had great respect for Sufism and for its followers, amongst whom was Rumi's father. This lasted until the theologian and philosopher Fakhreddin Razi and his friends succeeded in influencing the *sultan* and turning him against Sufism – so much so that the master of the great Sufi Fariduddin Attâr, Mecdeddin Baghdadi, was sentenced to death and atrociously slaughtered before having his body thrown into the river. This is why Rumi's father, in the face of so much contempt and hatred for Sufism, decided to leave the country. According to Shamsoddin Ahmad Aflâki, the *sultan*, fearing uprisings from the people who greatly revered Bahaeddin Valad, begged him to change his mind. This was in vain. Bahaeddin Valad left Balkh and made his way towards Mecca, accompanied by his very young son Celâleddin Rumi.

Aflâki states that this departure forewarned great catastrophes, such as the invasion by Genghis Khan's armies, who completely devastated the country, leaving no trace of life behind them. Some historians give a different version: for them, Valad left Balkh and Trans-Oxiana because he had a foreboding of the arrival of Genghis Khan's troops. I prefer the first version. It is said in the Qur'an: 'As long as you are amongst them, they will not be punished.' This verse shows the belief in the divine protection of people who shelter a holy man. To them, no harm can come.

I stayed two days in Balkh with my Afghan friends, who had acquired some horses. Thus we could visit the surrounding area, where there are few living people but an abundance of mausoleums. Just as statues are erected in the memory of great men in the West, so in the East the tradition is to build tombs, which one is meant to visit to commemorate luminaries who are no longer alive. I do not remember the names of the mausoleums' occupants except – unforgettable to me – that of the prophet Suleyman. His tomb was an impressive building in the middle of a lake. To get there, it was necessary to make a crossing using the tire of a lorry onto which a plank was fixed. Drawn by a system of double ropes we could thus get to the little island and visit the tomb. Actually, it was unlikely that Suleyman had really been buried there; it was probably just a cenotaph.

Two caretakers lived on the island, and had as their only comforts a straw mattress thrown on the beaten earth and a miserable teapot. I spent the rest of the day with them, talking about this and that. They knew nothing of the rich history of their country or of Rumi. Genghis Khan's men had not only destroyed all traces of life, but even the shadow of all memory. Was this not even more serious than the fact of losing life? No longer to exist in the collective memory, no longer to know where you come from, and thus, who you are and where you are going, corresponds to complete annihilation.

I rejoined my friends at Mazar-e-Sharif, from where I was expecting to leave for Kabul. A dozen of them insisted on coming with me on the twelve-hour coach journey. They had brought baskets of food from which they fed me hard-boiled eggs, chicken and fruit during the whole trip. My only regret was not being able to spend my remaining money. I was not allowed to pay either for the hotel or the coach ticket.

Some years later, two of the young Afghans who had accompanied me to Kabul came to visit me in Istanbul. Unfortunately, we lost touch after the war between the Russians and the Afghans. In 1986, at the time of my first trip to Pakistan, when I found myself in Peshawar (where numerous refugees were assembled), I came across some of these friends from Mazar-e-Sharif. They had become *mujaheddin* (warriors).

TWELVE

Sheik Muzaffer and Sufism in the US

In a Sufi brotherhood, one of the central characters is the *pir* (master), which in Persian means 'the old one', or 'the ancient'. In North Africa, the word *muqaddam* or *murshid* is used for one who awakens, one who guides. The whirling dervishes consider Celâleddin Rumi as the *pir* of their brotherhood. Most brotherhoods bear the name of their founding master, but each one of them has known masters who did more than just perpetuate a tradition. Some played such a decisive role in the history of their brotherhood that their name was given to it. For instance from the Halveti brotherhood many others branches grew: the Celveti, Sumbuli, Cerrahi, etc.

These changes of names do not come in any way from the pride of any *sheik* whose wish for power was such that he would have wanted to give his name to the brotherhood. It is much more to mark a change in tone, a different 'taste', a 'perfume' corresponding to a different epoch. It is somehow, for us Muslims, like the process of the advent of the prophets. We believe in one God who sent messengers: prophets who simply proclaimed the Oneness of God. Each new prophet started a new religion, and its dogma lasted until the coming of its successor. This is how it can be said that Judaism took the name of Christianity (if one considers Jesus as a prophet), and Christianity took the name of Islam with the coming of the Prophet Muhammad. The coming of each new prophet does not invalidate the previous message. There is a kind of continuity when the next step is taken, which brings a new light.

The same process occurred in the history of the brotherhoods. The new *pir* to whom the brotherhood is connected (and which will eventually bear his name) does not in any away deny the founding *pir*. He remains faithful to him, whilst differentiating himself from him. He makes the brotherhood take a new step on the *tariqa* (the way).

The Mevlevi brotherhood is the only one that has never had a new branch since Rumi founded it seven centuries ago. It is hard to explain, as remarkable figures later appeared in this tradition, and yet not one changed its name. It must also be said that a century after Rumi, a very rigid organisation exercised a strict control on the brotherhoods under its authority.

Another reason for these changes of names was geographical distance. For instance, one brotherhood that had started in Khorasan and later came to Istanbul took the name of the master who had brought it there. Thus the Qadiri brotherhood, founded in Baghdad by Abdul Qader Geylani, having been brought into Turkey by Ismail Rumi, took in Istanbul the name of Rûmî, although everyone knew that this *tariqa* was originally Qadiri.

The Cerrahi brotherhood is one of the branches of the *tariqa halvetiya* lineage. Nureddin Cerrahi lived at the end of the seventeenth century. His *tekke* is at Edirnekapi in Istanbul. When the Sufi houses were closed in 1925, the *sheik* of this brotherhood was Fakhreddin Efendi. Three or four of his disciples remained faithful to him, amongst whom were Sefer Dal (the present *sheik*) and Kemal Baba. The master could no longer enter his own *tekke*. The door was heavily bolted. Like other *sheiks*, he took to gathering his disciples in a café, a bookshop or sometimes in a private flat. Yet in spite of being outside the traditional *tekke*, the hierarchy was strictly respected within the community.

One day, as he was walking through the *bazaar* of old books, Fakhreddin Efendi met Muzaffer Ozak, the librarian and honorary preacher of the small mosque in the Great Bazaar. The two men became friends, and thus the old bookstore where they met became a Sufi meeting place. Each day, sitting on small straw-covered stools, holding a glass of tea, a few disciples listened to readings or wise teachings.

When Fakhreddin Efendi died, Sheik Muzaffer succeeded him. One day, very calmly, he stood in front of the closed door of the *tekke* and, with a good kick, smashed the bolt. With about ten of his friends he lit the stove, cleaned the meeting room and settled in. The Cerrahiya *tekke* was reborn. This reopening created a shock in the Sufi circles of Istanbul. Muzaffer was not highly considered by the other *sheiks*. After all, he was only an *imam*, and he was not known as having either the understanding or the subtlety required for the *tariqa*.

I went to this reborn *tekke* many times. The feeling there was very different from that which I had known in other *tekke* I had been to with my father. To the Nasuhi *tekke*, the Uzbek *tekke* or the Rufaiya *tekke* came rather well-educated people who all appreciated 'classical' literature or music. They tended to consider the Cerrahiya *tekke* as the meeting place of uncultured rug dealers from the Great Bazaar.

Personally, I found the atmosphere warm and pleasant around Sheik Muzaffer. Cheerfulness emanated from his presence, and he was also an extraordinary storyteller. He enjoyed life, had an imposing stature and liked to emphasise the slightest detail in the formalities of Sufi tradition. Unlike the other *sheiks* who gave no importance to their clothes, he liked to wear the robe, belt and turban proper to his function. This made him all the more impressive.

Together with his disciples, in order to divert the attention of the authorities, he founded an association with the official aim of protecting and caring for the master Nureddin Cerrahi's mausoleum, and to this was added the teaching of Sufi 'folklore'.

Even on the days most celebrated in Islam, there were scarcely more than thirty people in this place. Its members used to smoke a lot and drink many glasses of tea while listening to Sheik Muzaffer, who enchanted them with his talent as a speaker.

There I discovered an aspect of Sufism which was very different from that which my parents had shown me. Moreover, I had the satisfaction of having made this discovery by myself. It was a great joy for me, during Ramadan, to stay with Sheik Muzaffer late at night. After the breaking of the fast and the prayer in the *tekke*, he would go out with his circle of friends, stroll in the streets or settle in a café in front of the university. There, sitting on small stools, we smoked the *nargile* and had soft drinks and sweetmeats while listening to his stories.

Many years later, when I had been living in France for some time and was becoming recognised as a musician, Sherif Khaznadar asked me to organise the participation of a Turkish group of Sufi musicians. That year, the programme of the Rennes festival was centred on Sufi music from different countries such as Egypt and Syria. My friend Nezih Uzel and I proposed to Sheik Muzaffer that we should participate.

Although this was a fascinating and new experience for me, the organising of it cost me a great deal of effort and expense. At the time, neither Nezih nor I saw this demanding activity as a full-time job. Each participant was to receive 1,500 *francs*. This was true for me as well as for all the members of the community who were to perform. As the budget of the festival was restricted, its directors decided to accommodate all the members of the community in a dormitory at the University of Rennes. Sheik Muzaffer's disciples did not accept that their master should be accommodated in such uncomfortable conditions. After many discussions it was agreed that the *sheik* could go to a good hotel.

Unfortunately for me, I had not taken certain traditions into account and this proved to be very costly. Each morning, custom required that all disciples come to kiss the master's hand as he woke up. Inevitably, this led to an invitation for all to have tea in the hotel dining room. As I was the one who organised their stay, it was taken for granted that I was to pay the enormous bill for all the tea that had been ordered. When they left, my salary as the organiser hardly covered these expenses, which it was my mistake not to have foreseen.

A strange anecdote, related to this stay in Brittany, comes back to mind. A dear friend of mine, Pierre Zuber, proposed a visit to the monastery of Mont Saint-Michel (he knew the Father Superior there). Very happily, I rented a coach and we all went together to pay a visit to the monks. There were many of us, as some of our friends from Paris who felt close to Sufism had come to Rennes for the festival and joined us.

We were welcomed by the abbot of the monastery who, after offering us tea, wished to make a welcome speech, which he asked me to translate. In short, he said more or less the following: 'Do you know, gentlemen, that I had my first contact with Islam with a plate? As a child, I was staying with my grandmother and slept in a bed over which there was a plate which I was always afraid would fall on my head. It was a plate made of earthenware decorated with a strange script. Later on I learned its meaning: "Allah". Fortunately, this plate never fell on my head.'

Even before he heard the translation of the abbot's words, Sheik Muzaffer – who did not understand a single word of French – stood up and gave me a parcel which he asked me to give to the abbot. 'Offer this to the gentleman,' he said, 'it is a big earthenware plate on which "Allah" is written. Tell him to hang it over his bed. God will protect him.' Astonishment could be seen on the faces of the participants who knew both languages. As for the abbot, once he understood he was stupefied, and remained speechless.

Tosun Bayrak, a Sufi *sheik* in New York, came especially to Rennes from the US to invite Sheik Muzaffer. It was not easy at the time to get out of Turkey; the trip to France thus represented an opportunity for Sheik Muzaffer to go directly to the US. This is how, together with about fifteen companions, he flew from Rennes to New York. What happened during that stay is not known, but he was invited again the following year.

In 1980, at Sheik Muzaffer's strong insistence, I participated in one of these 'missionary' tours. What I saw was most surprising. Amongst the newly recruited disciples was Philippa de Menil, an heiress to the Schlumberger family oil fortune. Her presence represented considerable financial support. Philippa and her husband Heiner Friedrich were then renamed 'Feriha' and 'Haidar'. This extremely rich family gave a lot of money to Sheik Muzaffer. They also offered him an imposing chauffeur-driven limousine, as well as luxurious cars for his close disciples.

Tosun, the American *sheik*, had the ambition of becoming the only representative of Sheik Muzaffer in New York, and thus to gain control of the community that was being formed. Furthermore, he made sure that he was the indispensable intermediary between the disciples and Sheik Muzaffer. Philippa and Heiner, who wanted to make a large donation to the community, told Sheik Muzaffer about this situation. He called Tosun at once and reprimanded him sharply for his unacceptable conduct. He asked him to keep out of the management of the community's affairs. After this memorable outburst, Philippa's family offered Sheik Muzaffer a magnificent property near New York. The following year, the Schlumberger family rented a building which was transformed into a mosque (called Masjid al-Farah) and decided to promote Sheik Muzaffer's community. With this in view, every year around forty people from Istanbul were invited, accommodated and highly paid.

A tour of the largest cities of the US was organised for them, but the aim had nothing to do with culture. They were not meant to give paying performances to the public, but rather to offer the opportunity to as many people as possible to listen to and discover the master, free of charge, simply in order to increase the number of disciples. Many meetings with communities of various mystical interests were also organised with a purely proselytising aim.

I could not bear this disgusting and crude proselytism for long. Members of the *sheik's* entourage were acting like disciple-hunters. Anyone who seemed to show an interest in his discourses was at once taken to see him and introduced as someone who wished to become a Sufi. It was a pitiful comedy. One day they introduced a young man who was the subject of much gossip, as he was the son of an American oil tycoon. They did so well that they ended up convincing him to become a disciple of Sheik Muzaffer, who did not only accept him as such but made him a *sheik* at once. With this title, he also bestowed on him the right to wear the clothes and the headdress of a master. The poor young man, who could not have understood much of what was happening to him, invited the whole community to his parents' place in San Francisco. There, in a sumptuous estate overlooking the Pacific Ocean, we were entertained in a grand marble hall. As an army of waiters dressed in waistcoats busily attended us, the young man introduced his new master to his parents and friends. A *zikr*, a ceremony and music were performed. Some time later, I gathered that this young man had met the Dalai Lama, to whom he made a donation of 500,000 dollars, and had become a Buddhist ...

In San Francisco, for fear of losing my respect for Sheik Muzaffer, I preferred not to pursue this missionary tour and asked him to allow me to return directly to Paris. I had the impression that he had let himself be trapped by a situation over which he no longer had any control. In the end, he appeared more interested in material comfort than in spiritual teaching. The devotion with which he was surrounded had made him lose all common sense. This is how, one day in a hall in San Francisco, dressed in his imposing traditional costume, he told the audience of his great sadness for the awful attempt on the life of his 'brother' President Ronald Reagan. During an interview on the radio he took an inappropriate political position. He aggressively accused the Arabs of colluding with 'atheists' (the Soviets) with the view to making war against the 'Men of the Book' (the Jews of Israel). The speech revealed his confused and simplistic understanding of politics. My great admiration for him was increasingly put into question by his discourses. I could not understand why this man, in going beyond his role, was following a path which was not his own and in so doing was making a fool of himself. The excessive amount of money and power had thrown him into a kind of decadence, which was very distressing. Nevertheless, the number of disciples of Sheik Muzaffer continued to grow year after year.

After the military *coup* in Turkey, the ban on Islamic activities was intensified, as well as the strengthening of secular nationalism and the relentless fight against the Turkish Communist movement. The so-called freedom granted democratically to political parties other than General Kenan Evren, the leader of the *coup* and the country, did not exist.

Sheik Muzaffer's comings and goings between the US and Turkey made the Turkish authorities see him as an important man, and they granted him great privileges. He boasted that he could now call General Evren 'my brother Kenan'. After Sheik Muzaffer's death, his 'brother Kenan' gave the extraordinary authorisation for him to be buried in the seventeenth-century Nureddin Cerrahi mausoleum. This peremptory decision totally contradicted a 1925 law stipulating that no one could be buried in a monument from the Ottoman period.

Nowadays, the Cerrahi brotherhood is directed by Fakhreddin Efendi, the true successor of the last *sheik* of this brotherhood before the *tekke* were closed. There again, however, the increasing number of disciples in this community makes it the prey of various political interests that could take advantage of the dynamism present in some Muslim circles. This is also the case for many other 'Sufi movements' which have appeared in recent years.

THIRTEEN

The Place of the Traditional Musician Today

There was an emperor in China who was a great lover of the arts. He invited the most important painters in his empire to his palace, and organised a competition to decide who was the best amongst them. At the end of the competition there were two finalists, one Chinese, one Byzantine. The walls of a large hall were divided into two equal areas for each of the two contestants, and a large sheet was stretched across the middle of the hall to separate them.

Each day the Chinese artist asked for a hundred different colours in order to accomplish his work. The Byzantine artist asked for nothing. The competition came to an end, and the emperor went to the hall to admire the work of the two artists and to decide which one was best. The Chinese artist had produced a remarkable painting, the likes of which had never been seen before. When the curtain was pulled back in order to judge the work of the Byzantine painter, the emperor was surprised to see that the walls were blank. But they had been rendered so smooth and so shiny that they reflected to infinity the painting of the Chinese artist.

This story from Rumi's *Mesnevî* shows how art at its highest level is the expression of a wish to discover, in the depths of ourselves, that the reflection of life around and within us is a work of art in itself. And what work of art can be as subtle as the divine creation?

The aim is for the work of an 'accomplished man' to be the reflection of nature, of the universe that surrounds him. But the 'accomplished artist' must beforehand acquire the technique, the skill to express himself. Unfortunately, the more artistic language becomes sophisticated and inaccessible, the less the artist has time to develop himself inwardly. Very often contemporary European art does not reflect the beauty of the divine creation, but rather the problems buried in the very depths of the artist. Furthermore, such artistic language tends to become incomprehensible and inaccessible to most people.

In the recordings of the improvisations by my grandfather, amongst others, one hears that he only uses the range of a fifth. In spite of this economy, in the ten or fifteen minutes during which his improvisations last, the musical phrases are never repeated, and one is more touching than the other. Musicians of today use several octaves, several modes, several modulations, but their improvisations over the same amount of time only relate to a simple demonstration of their technical skill.

Listening to the *qanun* as it is played today, and to archival recordings of the same instrument, one hears the most implausible technical prowess achieved by contemporary musicians. This is completely contrary to the masters who, forty years ago, played *qanun* with the greatest simplicity, without ever making a display of their skill. And yet from the recordings they left, an emotional force emanates which has never been equalled in today's interpretations. The truth is that virtuosity alone cannot replace an execution that is simpler but rich in knowledge and full of imagination. I am reminded of having seen people weeping at the sound of a voice, or of an instrument being played with a moving simplicity, during the *sama'* which unfolded in the *tekke* of the past. Now we seem to have lost this feeling, the true spirit of this music.

Let me tell another story:

One day a sultan asked his vizier to find him someone who could do what nobody else could. After a long search, the vizier brought him a man who could, at a distance, throw a thread into the eye of a needle. He accomplished this marvel several times at greater and greater distances. The admiring sultan then said to his vizier: 'Give the man 100 gold pieces and 100 blows with a stick.' The performer was delighted with the gold but astonished by the beating. The sultan then said to him: 'The 100 gold pieces are for accomplishing this feat, the 100 blows are to punish you for having wasted your time on something so futile.'

The same goes for art. It is not distinguished any more from vulgar tricks. The impossible is not always the beautiful. Moreover, beauty is not necessarily impossible.

I would like to rediscover the authentic knowledge of the old masters, and above all, to find again the force, the human quality behind the traditional music of the East. I have set myself the task to rediscover, and to share amongst the artists with whom I collaborate, this strength which is lost today. I wish music to be not simply entertaining, but to bring about a profound feeling shared between those who listen and those who give it life.

In the East, the artistic tradition has never changed. A sense of continuity can be felt, if only superficially, between a work composed in the fourteenth century and that of a contemporary composer. In the literary field, poets have always developed the same themes: the rose, the thorns, the nightingale … It might appear that ideas and thoughts have hardly changed in the last seven centuries. This is a wrong idea! The garden of roses, the thorns, the nightingale, are only words. They can express distinct emotions and meanings. The same thing can be said of music. The modal system of the *maqam* has remained the same, but the genius of the composers, within this common ground, has brought a great diversification of this language.

As I see it, Europe has always swung between balance and imbalance. When it believed it had found a truth, quite another truth appeared soon after to invalidate it. New currents of thought were born as a reaction to the ideas that had just preceded them. Europe has no philosophical, religious or artistic stability. This diversification can appear as a richness. The East and the Middle East, from Japan to the threshold of Europe, has not known this kind of diversification. Is it because the East has found, or had the impression of having found something, and abandoned any thought of searching further? Is it because the West is constantly looking for that which it still does not know, even if it means abandoning it once it is found? These are questions I ask myself. But it is obvious that East and West complement each other, each having so great a need for the richness of the other.

Art cannot be the exclusive prerogative of a country, a nation or a people. It belongs to the whole of humankind, even more so nowadays when the cultural heritage of the world can be appreciated as never before, especially in the West. I am always full of admiration for the fact that Buddhists, for example, can find in Europe works which no longer exist in Tibet, or that Muslims can find in the great libraries of Paris or London manuscripts that they can no longer access in their native countries. A lover of traditional music can find recordings or texts on music far more easily in Europe than in their countries of origin.

People of our time are filled with a mass of information to which their parents had no access. If the bee only gathers the pollen of roses, it will make rose honey; if it gathers the nectar of acacias, it will make acacia honey. Just like a bee, an artist can take in a great variety of food, some even coming from very far away. He or she can make the culture of the past, of the present time, of the whole world, his or her own. Is this honey, or the work of contemporary artists, related to this rich potential, of which they are the result? I do not think so. Perhaps people today are saturated with all the possibilities available to them. On the other hand, there are many countries which remain within their own cultural limits.

Nowadays Turks, for instance, have the opportunity to be nourished by a diverse culture, but they generally only take in cultural leftovers from the West – the most trivial and commercial products of a consumer society. The West has the finest, richest, most perfumed food, but is rarely nourished by it. If the West produced what really corresponded to its possibilities, perhaps the non-Western countries could find their own 'perfumes'.

Cultural aims in the world are confused. However, culture is indispensable for everyone's development. It allows people to find their places, to consider and assimilate what exists beyond their usual horizons. I repeat: whoever is able to appreciate Rumi in Turkey must equally be able to appreciate Shakespeare. Just as in Europe, whoever loves Shakespeare should be able to appreciate Rumi without considering his work as belonging to 'Eastern folklore'; a Western music lover should feel the need to discover 'classical' music belonging to different horizons. To be sensitive to music is to be able to be sensitive to all sorts of music without excluding any, without limiting oneself to a specific colour.

However, the point is not to become prey to what is generally called 'global culture'. In order to enrich the cultural memory of humankind, it is essential for everyone to have access to the data of their own cultural heritage. In order to be able to appreciate different cultures, it is fundamental to be familiar with one's own. The great cultural sources of humanity must be rediscovered and made accessible to all. Beforehand, however, it is necessary to destroy the 'Eurocentric' attitude, to no longer see the world exclusively from the European viewpoint.

People are the same everywhere. Only their reactions differ, according to the civilisations to which they belong. It is interesting to see how an American person in love shows this love, or how a Chinese person expresses the same emotion. The feeling is the same, only the way in which it is expressed is different. The common denominator is humankind itself. Art must correspond to what a person knows. The artist must be one who fully lives the situations, and the emotions which any person can experience. Artists must share with others, through their art, what they have experienced. Culture, art, is the vehicle for all these shared attractions. People today have the extraordinary opportunity to access to feelings, emotions or ideas experienced by inhabitants of the four corners of the world.

There is no such thing as 'Sufi music'. There is only music listened to by Sufis. If Rumi were amongst us, he, who wrote so many poems about the *ney*, might have been touched by the sound of a saxophone. Who knows if he would not have written a poem about this instrument? Art must not be fixed in the past, or it becomes dried-up tradition, comparable to a dead language. If an artist with a traditional heritage truly lives his or her art, it is contemporary art expressed in a specific language.

> One day a man walked into a wine bar and ordered a glass of wine. He specifically said to the waiter, 'When you bring my glass, bang it strongly on the table and say, "Here is your wine".' The waiter agreed to this strange request, but asked the reason for it. The man then answered, 'When I ask you to bring me wine, intellectually I know that you are going to bring it. When you do, I shall see it, and my eyes will be happy. Then I will enjoy it, and my taste buds and my nose will be happy. I wondered what would be left for my ears.'

Humans live as if though locked up in a concrete room with five openings. These represent their only contact with the outside world. Music, what is seen by the eyes, what is tasted, what is smelled and what is touched are the only opportunities to escape this prison. The more the material aspect of life weighs on us, the more one forgets how enclosed one is, as well as the opportunities one has to free oneself. People need to be able to hear music which can console them while in jail and remind them that they can be free, just as they need to see works of art which fill them with joy and deep memories, and to touch, or to smell delicious scents. At all times, different artistic expressions have played such a role.

Nowadays, however, all these arts only serve as entertainment in the prison. Although this entertainment momentarily allows the prisoners to forget their condition, in no way does it remind them of the state of freedom. It is just what Rumi means in a poem about the *ney*, when he considers this instrument as a remedy. It brings relief to the one who suffers, but it is also a poison in the sense that it reminds the prisoners that they have lost their freedom, and does not give them the possibility of recovering it. Thus jail only becomes more unbearable.

But what is this state of freedom? Freedom means not to be limited by one's own nature. The mission of art has always been to remind people that life is ephemeral and that they must find the means to be relieved of the weight of feeling that this implies. Art is not mere distraction, but a deep reflection on the human condition. It seems to me that this is true for all civilisations. Global culture, which stems from the commercial world in which we live today, despises the greatest mission of art.

There certainly exists a common need in all human beings: to find some joy, some freedom in this world which is a prison. Nowadays this aim, which belongs to most artistic expression, is not made use of as it should be. If it were, I am convinced that a conscious person, whatever his or her cultural language, could share any sound, any image, any smell, without considering himself or herself first as a Turk, a French person, an Arab, a Persian.

As Rumi says in his poem, the *ney* is a companion to all those who rejoice, as well as to those who weep. With my *ney* I join other musicians, classical, contemporary or jazz, with whom I try to share my own experience. Maybe there are some who think that I have betrayed my cultural heritage. To these traditionalists, who are terrified of losing the values to which they are attached, I would say that if one wishes for these values to be lasting, one must learn to share them; to relate to other values coming from different cultures. If I have been able to confront myself without damage to other civilisations, to other musical languages, it is because I am convinced that I am living my own heritage to the full.

FOURTEEN

Transmission

From the Eighties onward, a small circle of enthusiasts who had attended the concerts and Sufi ceremonies open to the public gathered around me to study Sufi music and literature. Meetings spontaneously took place in the small studio where I lived at the time. As the number of people showing interest was growing, an association was formed for practical issues, such as the renting of a proper place. Most of those who came were students or academics.

As work on the music started, one of the first problems I had to face was to provide a *ney* for each one of them. I solved that by making *neys* from hard plastic tubes. Inexpensive and easy to manufacture, this makeshift instrument was good enough for beginners. Some time later, while giving a concert at the Abbaye of Senanque, I found a small river nearby, lined with reeds. With one of my pupils, Stéphane Gallet, I was able to make flutes worthy of the name. For the mouthpieces, which are traditionally made of horn, we found a synthetic material. All the pupils having now been given *neys*, I began to teach the technique. Few of these students had previously been taught any music. Most of them were beginners, and moreover, beginners in Turkish music. Passion and patience brought results which could be felt after a certain time.

Some students, returning from a trip to Turkey, brought back *tanburs, ouds* and *kemençes*. With these new instruments the teaching diversified. Definite results were obtained: several students acquired enough knowledge to make it their profession. A few of them, starting from this base of classical Turkish music, created new compositions. This was the case for the Turkish Blend band, which plays a kind of jazz fusion. Others amongst my students composed music for theatre and ballet.

Little by little, this activity became known in other circles. Our group included *maghrebins*, students from the third generation of North African immigrants who were looking for a cultural identity. They did not come as a result of their passionate encounter with Sufi music. It was by word of mouth that they learned of the existence of our association. I could do very little towards answering their need for a cultural identity. In fact, apart from one person, no Turkish immigrant was ever a student of mine. I could see that they, and immigrants in general, were only vaguely interested in the universal values which could emanate from their own cultures. Artistically they were motivated by music for mass consumption, such as *raï* or *arabesk*, the latter a popular Turkish-Arab music mixed with electronic Western sounds.

Having become my pupils, the young *maghrebins* had to confront such sophisticated literature and music that it seemed beyond them. It was more difficult to teach them about their own cultural origins than to teach the young French students whose motivation seemed greater and who listened more enthusiastically. To understand Rumi is not the same as understanding Turkish, Persian or Arabic. Beyond the language, beyond the culture, my aim was to transmit a way of thinking through a music and a literature, which could have a universal influence. This could only be received by those who were in accord with this direction. It was the same for the teaching of music. Extremely sophisticated phrases, intervals and rhythms were difficult to communicate to these young *maghrebins* whose ears were somewhat 'corrupted' by the sounds they were used to hearing.

My travels to India, Pakistan and countries in the Arab world allowed me to observe that the classical culture of these various regions knew no frontiers, contrary to the 'classical' culture of Italy, Germany, England or France which, through relating to each other, constitute European culture. A classical Islamic culture, which was not specifically Turkish, Persian or Arab, has existed. This can be verified through the example of Abdul Qader Meragî, a composer who lived in the fifteenth century. Born in Azerbaijan, he established himself at the court in Baghdad, then belonged to the house of Sultan Bayezid in Turkey, to whom he dedicated one of his works. After the war of Angora with Tamerlane, he was made a prisoner in Samarkand and then, as a follower of Tamerlane, he returned to Baghdad. Abdul Qader Meragî is one of those musicians who brought their talent from court to court. His works were appreciated by the learned circles of all the potentates with whom he lived. Another example is the composer Hussein Baikara, grandson of Tamerlane, who was the *sultan* of Khorasan in today's Afghanistan. His musical compositions are part of the classical Turkish repertoire and were played at the Ottoman court. Today he is probably largely forgotten in Afghanistan. Is his work Turkish or Afghan? Surely both one and the other.

There were many exchanges of artists between Iran and Turkey, and their works are now part of the Turkish repertoire. During his expedition to Revan, Sultan Murad IV – a great lover of music – became a friend of its governor, Yusuf Gân, who was surrounded by well-known musicians. After his conquest of the city, Sultan Murad took Emir Gân and all his court with him to Istanbul. The *sultan* had a palace built for him on the Bosphorus in a district which still bears his name, Emirgân (a Turkish distortion of 'Emir-i-Qun'). A whole repertoire dating from that time is an integral part of classical Turkish music.

Conversely, all Persian poems in Ottoman times were meant to be accompanied by classical music. Poems by Saadi or Hafez were set to music by Turkish composers. Certain poets in the Ottoman court considered it essential to write in Persian. There were many political exchanges as well as cultural ones between the Persian and Ottoman courts. The prolific correspondence between Shah Ismail and Sultan Yavuz Selim, at the beginning of the sixteenth century shows how close the literary and musical exchanges between the two empires were. This all-embracing cultural heritage may have suffered in the twentieth century from the creation of nation-states, which wanted to differentiate themselves through their own cultures.

The research undertaken by Europeans, who unearthed the authenticity of these cultures, brought to light the impoverishment they had suffered. The political borders drawn during this century have clipped their wings. Art, literature and music are beyond the concept of nation. My own cultural field includes the Balkans, India (many *qawwali* come from Rumi's poems), the Arab world including the Maghreb and Romania (birthplace of Prince Dmitri Kantemir, who transcribed a great deal of Turkish classical music). Nowadays, *peshrev* (preludes) of Cemil Bey are still interpreted in Tunisia or Algeria. There are many traces of a classical culture common to all these countries. I dream of a shared wish to revive it, without any consideration for the political borders from the Indian continent to the Maghreb. ˙

It can also be said that music, as a means of expression, goes further than its context. It can be appreciated even without the knowledge of underlying bonds between civilisations.

In Europe the teaching of classical music interpretation does not allow for the development of improvisation. Music requires very advanced study. Harmony and counterpoint generate a common expression, not an individual one. A clarinetist pupil of mine came to see me after having studied for ten

years at a conservatory, and asked me to teach him to improvise. He told me
that, to his great regret, he could not express himself musically without the
help of a score.

A pianist must sustain his practice and have a thorough theoretical
knowledge in order to undertake complex interpretations. But this same
musician is usually disorientated if asked to improvise; in contrast, a jazz
musician, without theoretical training, possesses an artistic instinct sufficiently
developed to allow him to perform work of great quality. Whereas Europe is
highly developed in terms of musical technique, it has lost a great deal with
regard to the capacity to improvise. But young French people who came to
seek musical instruction from me, even with no previous knowledge of music,
were in the end able to express themselves both individually and collectively
through this flute whose resonance had touched them. From the start, they
could manifest their emotions much more easily than with classical music.

The recordings I made in France became known in North Africa. One
incident deeply touched me: a young man from Tangiers, Abdelouahid
Senhaji, who was a mechanic by trade, had been given one of my albums and
fell in love with the sound of the *ney*. He wrote to me. I did not meet him, but
had other recordings of mine sent to him and offered him a *ney*. With some
advice given from afar, a few years later he was able to perform on Moroccan
television. He started a group to play Sufi music inspired by my albums. Today
he is regularly sent abroad by the Moroccan Ministry of Culture to represent
the Sufi music of his country. The one meeting I had with him and his friends
took place quite by chance at the airport in Vienna where I had stopped on
my way to perform in Istanbul. They themselves were going to Bosnia, where
they were giving a concert. This is how I suddenly found myself surrounded
by a group of Moroccan musicians who recognised me from photographs.
Even if our meeting lasted only about ten minutes, it allowed me to realise the
musical influence I can have in a country whose culture has much in common
with ours.

As for the association I created in Paris, it took part in the Nineties in
Franco Battiato's opera *Genesis*. This composer, a great lover of Mevlevi
music, invited me to collaborate with him for parts of his work. He was keen
to include a ceremony of whirling dervishes and therefore asked for my help
to bring a suitable group from Turkey. It seemed inappropriate to me for
a real dervish community to perform, so I proposed to teach some people
from the association the dance of the whirling dervishes. In this way, this part
would be integrated in his work and would not become an exploitation of a
tradition seven centuries old. He agreed with me. I directed a workshop for

a fortnight within the association to teach the *sama'* to those who wished to take part. Since then, alongside the association, a group of people was formed that often performs the ceremony according to the rules. They sometimes even take part in the ceremonies of the Turkish whirling dervishes who have accepted them in their midst. There is a strong attraction to traditional music for a whole new generation in my native land. Since the Eighties I have met many young and talented musicians who practise either an instrument or the art of singing. With them, I formed a group which has happily developed to the present day.

It is important to underline the differences between the approach to music of my father's generation and that of the young generation with whom I work nowadays. The older generation I knew in my youth, and with whom I was happy and honoured to play, consists of well-known names in classical Turkish music. Most of these musicians were convinced then that the music they played represented the end of an era. They saw the Ottoman culture as obsolete, whether from a literary or musical point of view, and saw themselves almost as the guardians of a museum of antiquity. They only played for a very restricted audience and believed that the only future course for this music, with its rich past, was to adapt to more contemporary ways of expression. They also thought it necessary to introduce polyphony into classical traditional music, and for their interpretation to come closer to European music. To this effect they advocated, for instance, the use of the tempered scale. They also wanted to make the *kemençe*, a bow instrument, sound like a violin; as the *kemençe* is made with three gut strings, they added a fourth, using a metallic one to obtain a sound they believed would be nearer to that of a violin. The new generation of musicians, aged between twenty-five and thirty, tries to rediscover the original authenticity of classical music – so they use *kemençes* with three gut strings.

Unfortunately, the interpretation for the singer could not follow this same wish to go back to the source. The public address systems which are always used everywhere make it possible even for very weak voices to be heard, whereas in the past only singers of real quality could project their voice as far as they needed to. Furthermore, literature changed with the modernisation of the Turkish language, and singers find it very difficult to interpret it so that it can be appreciated. Many artists have taken to adapting the text of classical songs to our time with short and more and more popular melodies, always accompanied, however, by traditional instruments.

The older generation had a deep knowledge of the old repertoire. Consequently, their improvisations could vary greatly. In comparison, the new generation is poorer in regard to melodic phrasing, even if they have reached perfection in the technical mastery of the instruments. This loss may perhaps be due to the constant listening to melodies which are so much under European influence that the authentic colour of the phrasing in the *maqam* systems is disappearing more and more. The *qanun*, a stringed instrument, ends up sounding like a harp, and the *oud* like a classical guitar.

For several years, I have been trying to bridge the richness in improvisation of old times and the technical qualities of the instruments and voices of today.

FIFTEEN

The Fountain of Separation

This story can be found in the Indian tradition:

An old man was travelling with a young disciple. Tired from walking, the old man stopped under a tree and, pointing to a village in the distance, he asked his disciple to bring him back some water in a jug, which he gave him. The young man took the jug and walked towards the village. Once there, he went to the fountain which, at that time of the day, was very much in demand by many women who came to fetch water for their households. He noticed a beautiful young girl and at once fell madly in love with her, so much so that he forgot all about the jug and the old man waiting for him under the tree.

He followed the young girl, and for several days walked around her house like a lost soul. The father of the young girl went to discover the reason for this strange behaviour; the young man told him of his love for the young girl, and asked if he could marry her. The father granted his permission, and the couple married and had several children.

Some years later, the oldest of the couple's sons asked leave to seek his fortune in the world at large. The disciple, his father, gave him his blessing. Year after year, each one of his children asked if they could leave home. Then his father-in-law and his mother-in-law died, and so did his wife. He found himself on his own. One day, as he was passing in front of the fountain, feeling sad, he suddenly remembered the jug, the water and his master whom he had forgotten under the tree. He ran to his house, looked for the jug, found it, filled it with water and rushed to the tree – sitting quietly there was the old man, who welcomed him, saying simply, 'Son, I was beginning to worry!'

I like this story very much. It describes so well the distractions, the aberrations that line the road of our lives. As we are, all of us walk around the 'Fountain of Separation' until the moment when we become aware of our *raison d'être*. Life then takes on another meaning. This fountain truly exists. It is the departure point towards an unknown place. In the past, it was in the Asian quarter of Istanbul, between Üsküdar and Kadikoy, the symbolic point of arrival and departure for the East. Parents and friends accompanied most of the pilgrims headed for Mecca, and they would then start their long journey on their own. I have myself often been accompanied up to this symbolic fountain by my family and my friends. Today, as the West has no more geographical limits and the world is tending to become a boundless globe, the fountain of separation is within me like the frontier of somewhere unknown.

Many Sufi masters taught that life is just a deviation, a wandering in front of eternity. Rumi said it consists of three days: childhood, youth and maturity. I am at the dawn of my third day. But, after all, as Rumi himself says, death is only a birth. A child in his mother's womb feels so good that he does not wish to leave it. Birth, as I said at the beginning of this book, is a catastrophe, an apocalypse, but one gets used to this life to the point of no longer wishing to leave it. Death, this other apocalypse, will perhaps open on to a wonderful unknown.

SIXTEEN

Islam, Sufism and the Modern World

Regarding the question of human beings, it is possible to consider three dominant themes: the relationship of a person to their nature, the relationship of a person with others and the relationship of a person to the divinity in which they believe. These three themes appear in most religions, and particularly in the religions of the Book.

The relationship of person to their own nature belongs to the domain of wisdom. This is the Greek principle, 'know yourself and you will know the universe and the gods'. The same was said by the Prophet of Islam, bringing to it the additional dimension of one God: 'he who does not know himself will not know his God'. The vast theme of self-knowledge has been a focus in Sufism as in many other spiritual disciplines. People, very often, are prisoners to the demands of their own natures. This state brings confusion to their relationships with others and in the rapport with the divinity in which they believe. The struggle of a person over the demands of their own nature is primordial. As the Prophet said, there are two sorts of struggle: the small struggle against an outer enemy, and the great struggle in one's inner world, against the demands of one's own nature which must be overcome. This struggle has no limits.

The Prophet said, *mutu qable ente mutu* ('die before dying'); victory over one's own nature goes as far as total submission, without reaction, like a being a corpse. This struggle is different for everyone, because each nature is dominated by different demands. Bearing grudges; anger; ambition; egoism; vanity; desire; avarice – these are all faults that human beings must confront. Some of these demands of one's nature are considered essential qualities in some societies. There is no doubt that generosity is a quality, no doubt that certain innate gifts for art, or the skill to make something, are worthy qualities. It is necessary to leave behind all the vices or virtues inherent to human nature. As Rumi said in his *Mesnevî*, it is not a question of making a selection of colours (good qualities) or of getting rid of certain colours (vices). It is a question of being without any colour so that, at the opportune moment, a 'reflection' can fall upon one. At this stage, the colour that will manifest in a person will no longer belong to human nature but to divine nature. In Sufism, the wish is the same as in other teachings of wisdom: to go beyond the features of human nature.

As for the relationship of human beings with their surroundings (the family or the society of which they are part), injunctions can be found in many religions to help them act rightly. These commandments, which range from 'Thou shalt not kill' and 'Thou shalt not steal' to recommendations (as in Islam, for instance) on such matters as inheritance, are a search for the right attitudes to direct the relationship of a person with himself or herself as well as with others.

The relationship to divinity is in the domain of theology. Whether it is the product of humans or the fruit of revelation, it offers a description of the Divine endowed with specific qualities. For Islam and for the religions of the Book as a whole, God hears all, sees all, knows all, gives and takes away life. He is omnipotent; He will destroy this universe as He has created it and, at the end of time, humankind will appear before Divine Justice.

These three kinds of relationships in the tradition of Abraham are bound one to another. In the Islamic context, the struggle against one's own nature and the search for morality are undertaken in the name of God. In modern times, we tend more and more to depart from traditions which were based on religious principles of wisdom and virtue. For traditional societies, the result is disarray and a difficulty in adapting to new values. If one compares some of the moral values of traditional societies (such as humility or altruism) with those current in the West (such as individualism or systems which work by exploiting human weakness) in contrast to the old values whose aim was to create strong and just people, we find paradoxes which confront many communities. Take, for example, the insurance system, which in modern societies has an increasingly important place. Based on doubt and uncertainty about tomorrow, this system is the opposite of the religious proposal that people should have a certain trust in their futures. One could give many more examples of this contradiction between the two worlds, that of modernity and traditional societies based on religious values.

Many Western countries have gradually adapted to these social and ethical changes. In contrast, many non-European societies experienced this 'evolution' as a cultural shock, as it was often brutally imposed by a state which aimed at modernisation. The refusal to accept the products of Western consumer society, and the changes in mentality they provoke, leads to a withdrawal and to a reaction which today we call 'fundamentalism'. It represents rejection, a resistance on the part of certain layers of society in front of a civilisation considered to be destructive. After the fall of the Berlin Wall, the Western world found itself facing a Muslim civilisation – a large part of the world's population that, with no political culture, resists Western consumer society, which it considers immoral.

For some years, intellectuals have pondered the possibility of a reconciliation with the Islamic world, but the cultural, economic or political solutions have not given the desired results. Seen with hindsight, up to the start of the twentieth century, the Ottoman Empire was a federation of most of the Muslim countries. It had already attempted to put Western culture alongside Islamic tradition and was partly successful, especially in the urban society. At the end of the First World War, after the defeat of the Ottoman Empire, a large number of new states were created and claimed their own nationality: Iranian, Turkish and Arab, the latter across a mosaic of countries such as Egypt, Syria, Lebanon, Algeria, Iraq, Saudi Arabia, Yemen, Libya and Tunisia. Each of these states, to differentiate itself from the others, attempted to develop a culture of its own. This ranged from a linguistic specificity to the reconstruction of its history and, in another domain, nuances in religious lifestyle. They wished to play the card of disparity between all these recently created nations.

But the driving force behind the advance of these new states was, once again, the reconciliation of national characteristics with the modernity of the West. For many of the leaders of these countries, it was necessary to follow the steps of contemporary reality. Thus, a gulf was created between traditional rural society and the more progressive urban society, because the latter had more to do with the Western world. When rural populations began to migrate to the towns, they had great difficulty integrating with this new way of life. This put a brake on years of work by progressives, who had tried their best to steer the urban population in the direction of modernity.

Amongst all these countries the example of Turkey is, without doubt, the most significant because its attempts at Westernisation are the oldest. From Selim III (1761–1808) to the Republic of Mustafa Kemal Atatürk (1923), political choices were made with a view to Western modernisation.

In Mustafa Kemal's Republic, it was decided to completely transform the country, whatever the cost. This brought about a real revolution in Turkish society.

Since the Fifties, some political parties were seen to defend the rights claimed by the Muslim community. These religious demands were supported by people who were suffering as a result of the excesses of modernisation that had been imposed on them. The immigrants to the big towns saw it as a question of their identity. Paradoxically, in spite of their assimilation into an urban consumer society, they wished to retain a purely Islamic identity, which they considered to be the very foundation of their existence.

Faced with this resistance, the leaders hardened their attitude towards these people, and this provoked an even bigger opposition. In the search for a reconciliation between modernity and Islam, the intelligentsia and the progressive political movements came to consider Sufism, with its inherent tolerance, as a possible answer to the intolerance of Islamic fundamentalism, believing this could bring a cultural dimension to the destructive and brutal qualities of Islamism. Furthermore Sufism could serve to justify the differences between nations. It justified the idea of a Turkish, Iranian, Iraqi or Syrian Islam on the basis of the Sufis, poets or saints originating from each of these countries. Thus Rumi could become a Turkish national symbol, and Abdel Qader Geylani an Iraqi national symbol, in spite of the fact that nothing in their lives or writings could really be seen to justify a modern Islam or a nationalist tendency. One only has to read the great work of Fariduddin Attâr, *Memorial of the Saints*, to be convinced of this. The saintly lives of these first Sufis show how much they were attached to the prophetic tradition. Its artistic expression through dance, music and the underlying rich literature, as well as the many possible interpretations of Rumi's teaching, transformed the Mevlevi brotherhood into a platform proposing a 'modern' Islam.

Consequently, certain Turkish politicians wanted to manifest their inclination for a European modernisation along with their apparent wish to express their attachment to the cultural and mystical Islam. They went as far as attributing to Rumi a poem which was, in fact, of their own making, and this purely for the aim of election propaganda:

Yine gel yine gel her kim olursan yine gel
kafir ve putperest de olsan yine gel
bu dergahimiz ümitsizlik dergahi değildir
yüz kere tövbeni bozsan da yine gel

'Come, come back, whoever you are, come back
even if you are an infidel, atheist or idolater, come back.
Our threshold is not a threshold of despair
even if you have repented and betrayed your promise,
come back.'

Not finding in traditional Sufism the necessary arguments for modernity
and for a moderate Islam, the works of European Orientalists were used. A
new approach to the texts of Rumi arose from the works of the European
scholars. So, alongside traditional Sufism there appeared a version of Sufism
inspired by Western visions. For Westernised urban society this second version
offered possibilities for reconciling modernity and Islam. Thus it was that the
works of Rumi were diverted from their original meaning. The poetic language
which he adopts in his work cannot have the rigidity of a dogmatic text. It
remains a language open to the taste and understanding of each person. This
second version found a certain echo in Turkey amongst the intelligentsia. It
was instrumental in changing the authentic and traditional understanding of
the work of Rumi, and of the commentaries which had been made about his
work in previous centuries, as well as the understanding of Islam through his
teachings. In the context of the Festival of Konya, the different ways of re-
establishing the ceremony of the whirling dervishes became more and more
evident.

For all those who felt concerned for Sufism in general, and for the Mevlevi
in particular, it was difficult to think of continuing to assemble and perform
the ceremony under the patronage of the tourist office in Konya. Celâleddin
Çelebi, thirty-second descendant of Rumi, was called upon, as it was thought
that he could save the situation: his lineage justified his holiness. Furthermore,
he spoke French, and his European lifestyle influenced his 'modernity'. He
was also a confirmed adept of Turkish Freemasonry which, in the eyes of
certain people, proved his attachment to Republican values.

Çelebi was a typical example of those who took the commentaries on
Sufism of the European Orientalists literally, and pronounced them as
fundamental truths. Although this last descendant of Rumi wanted to increase
the interest which had arisen in Sufism and the dervishes, he only slavishly
repeated the more or less confused writings of some European Orientalists.
Some of his errors were based on their works. For instance, this is how the
ceremony of the whirling dervishes was considered to be the representation
of the movement of the stars turning around the sun (the *sheik* being the sun).
Çelebi perpetuated the theory found in the works of Eva Vitray-Meyerovitch.

In the same order of ideas one could marvel at the discovery of a poem written by Rumi in which it could be deduced that, long before Westerners, he had understood that the world was round; or to find certain data in the *Mesnevî* that makes it possible to conclude that, long before Freud, Rumi had discovered psychoanalysis, as he was able to cure certain patients suffering from mental illness by going back to the origins of their experience. One could multiply such examples *ad infinitum*.

Çelebi tried to make Rumi known again not as a Sufi but, as he called himself, a humanist. He established the Mevlana Foundation in Turkey. Several years later, he invited me to become its spiritual head; to this I replied that it was for him to fulfil that role. But quite obviously he preferred to stay in the background, not wishing in any way to become a man of *tariqa*. He wished to keep to a European view of Sufism. However, from his point of view, I was the man for that position: I had been brought up in a traditional Sufi family, played the *ney*, knew the customs of the *tariqa* and had also translated into French a work on the *Mesnevî*. My refusal to accept his proposal, and my independence from the centralisation that his foundation represented, meant that I was no longer acceptable to Çelebi and his entourage.

Some Islamic circles reacted against this approach. To begin with, they considered Mevlevi Sufism as heretical; then they wanted to retrieve it by making it conform to their own demands. Apart from tradition, and the modernised and Europeanised version of Sufism, a third version came to light. For the liberals, Rumi was a drunken poet who felt himself freed from all religious obligation and who had always been misunderstood by traditional Sufis; conversely, the Islamists made him into a man after their own image, a strictly pious man and a Muslim fundamentalist. They even went as far as to say that he had never advocated music or dance, and that it was pure heresy to pretend to the contrary.

Aware of this austere Sufism, a great number of rural communities which had emigrated to the cities ended up acquiring certain political weight. It became obvious that many Islamic political movements justified themselves through Sufism. Consequently, what remains of authentic Sufism now finds itself in great difficulty because, on the one hand, it is considered a threat to democracy and secularism and, on the other, as a threat to Muslim fundamentalism. It is regrettable that such a rich religious tradition has become misunderstood by so many. It seems logical that when adhering to a truth, one resents those who do not. Those who discover a truth would like to fight the whole world to make them discover it in turn.

To return to the three dimensions, humans and their nature, humans in relation to others and in relation to God: it is certain that at the root of everything, there is the fact of humans standing in relation to themselves. One must first acquire a soundness, a clarity in onself before this can influence one's surroundings. But we must not lose sight of the fact that all this evolves in the context of a relationship between humans and God. The notion of tolerance attributed to Sufism comes from the idea that one must be demanding towards that which concerns one's own nature and tolerant towards what is proper to others. In a society inclined towards religious values, the mistake is often made of wanting to transform one's surroundings before transforming oneself. It is the attitude of the ordinary person to demand from others that which he or she refuses to apply to himself or herself.

The institutionalisation that makes the religious message into a political issue presents a danger because the subjective dimension that allows everyone to go beyond their own nature, is lost. Numerous religions were thus transformed into a way to justify worldly passions, passions arising from human nature, when they should be giving people opportunities to overcome them.

All teaching, all awakening, is only possible through human relationships. It is a light which spreads from one person to another. We are not talking of institutions, books or traditions, but of people. From this perspective, Sufism holds an important place because it makes present that which was lived in the past, and brings to life that which has been considered in an academic way. It allows one not to distance oneself from revelation but, on the contrary, to live it. Very often the presence of 'he who is' goes beyond even the word. A living example can go beyond all religious teaching, all tradition.

Imagine a bird living in a cage kept on the balcony of its owner. Not having known any other life, it sees, one day, one of its fellow creatures flying quite free. This example, this model of freedom, leads it to question its own fate. The meeting of a seeker of truth with a Sufi, or a person living 'in freedom', is of the same nature as that of the caged bird which sees another bird flying freely. A decisive meeting goes far beyond the understanding of the truth that is given by books. At best, the aim of such readings can prepare for and lead to the recognition of the moment of meeting an enlightened person. Thus, in the sacred history of Islam, we can see the example of Umar, who, having decided to kill the Prophet, went into his house, sword in hand. As soon as he saw him, at first glance, he was instantaneously and radically transformed. Following this decisive meeting he became the fortieth true Muslim to immediately leave his own affairs in order to announce the prophetic message.

This mystical proselytising, whether religious or political, brings together communities of millions of followers today. Their success is surprising if we consider that many of the prophets only had in their time a limited number of faithful (twelve apostles for Jesus and forty companions for Muhammad). In the Sufi tradition the meeting of Rumi and his master Shams of Tabriz is another example illustrating such inner transformation.

Today the religious traditions, which have over the centuries acquired layers of hypocrisy, have become empty of meaning. They are often no more than superstition, beliefs based on misunderstandings. When these are imposed on whole societies, for many they are an obstacle to experiencing their own approach to the Truth. I am convinced that to live in the world, contrary to what many religious people think, is a necessity in the search for Truth, not as an obligation but from personal choice. Certain religious communities have started from a personal search and yet, in the course of their history, they end up by deviating from their original objective, like a flame swiftly extinguished. Islam existed in its original purity during the life of the Prophet and for the three following generations. Then wars and social unrest led to chaos. Thanks to certain wise Sufis, and the presence of enlightened figures such as Rumi, the flame of Islam was revived. In Sufism there is a right understanding that this continuity has taken place through such enlightened figures. They kept alive the divine message, not by virtue of new prophecies, but by serving as a link between prophets of the past and people of today. The search for Truth is not, in my opinion, a question of mass culture but a matter for the elite.

Furthermore, I do not believe in the spirit of compromise with regard to those who use Sufi literature as a means of reconciling the differences between religions, for this multiplicity is in itself an expression of divine will. It is rather like someone who suffers from seeing double; wanting to do away with that which is in front of them, they risk destroying everything, unable to distinguish what is true from what is false.

Here let me quote the words of Rumi: 'Religions are like candles. They are useful for finding one's way in the dark. We need their light to guide us.' The differences which occur are in the candles and not in one's inner light. The quarrels over the merits of this or that candle can only lead to misunderstanding, because they only take into account the means and not the end. Rumi continues: 'When day breaks and night is gone, it is ridiculous to hang on to one's candle. Its light is weak compared to that of the sun which represents Truth.'

If one considers that the wick of these candles represents the individual, one can speculate at long length on the form, forgetting that the sole purpose of any candle is to bring light. This is how many authentic traditions and legacies have deviated from their *raisons d'être*. And yet, deviant as they are, they are taken today as unquestionable sources. But 'it is not the cowl that makes the monk'. To belong to a spiritual dynasty (it is well known that the sons of a number of prophets were unbelievers), or to belong to a tradition, are no longer investitures to be trusted. Nowadays, many references to the tradition contradict their sources, as it happened for the whirling dervishes or Sufism in Turkey. And yet, it is more necessary than ever to go back to the beginnings and understand the original texts. To avoid being confused by the assertions of some 'living spiritual masters', one must not lose sight of the religious basis of Sufism. Sufi teaching requires the *shari'a* (strict respect of the Qur'an and the traditions of the Prophet). The *tariqa* (the way) leads to *hakikat* (truth) and *ma'rifat* (knowledge). Sufism cannot be understood without the belief in one God.

The conflict between modernity and religion exists also in the scientific field. Many consider today that a certain kind of obscurantism was started with religions refusing to recognise scientific discoveries. The Turkish intelligentsia thus accused religion of delaying the progress in technology. In Rumi's teaching, one can see that religion, far from being an obstacle to human reason, is a light which can guide it. For him, science gives the possibility to admire the subtleties created by God.

For something to exist, there must be a cause. The universe is a multiplicity of causes and effects which reverberate *ad infinitum*. The birth of a human being is an effect: the consequence of an intimate relationship between a man and a woman. Religions consider that this relation between cause and effect is created by God to vindicate humans at the level of their intelligence. It is up to man to know the effects and the causes of every phenomenon through science. Religions link all causes and effects in affirming that God is the cause of all causes. Following this thought, religions are not incompatible with scientific thinking; on the contrary, they must be its driving force. Science should lead to acquiring and admiring the subtlety of divine creation. Unfortunately, many religious people considered science as a sin, this human curiosity wishing to understand God's work. Although scientific thought often leads to atheism, it can also be at the origin of a quest for faith. Just as a cultural heritage allows for better living in modern times, Islam also is a necessary light in discerning present values. The Islamic credo begins with these words: *Eshhedu* ('I witness') *en lailahé* ('that there is no other God') *illa Allah* ('but Allah'). From negation, affirmation is born. It is necessary to deny all the forms of God invented by humans to affirm He who is One for all.

The conflict between the beliefs of modernists and traditionalists regarding science, and the bringing of Islam into the field of politics, both seem to me unfounded. There is in this battle a negative view of the epoch in which we live. Looking back, however, one can see that humankind has never known a peaceful, just, and true era. Conflict has existed throughout history, even at the time of the prophets, who never succeeded in correcting these 'erring ways'. The Prophet Muhammad said: 'This world is the paradise of the unfaithful, this world is the prison of the faithful.' It is hard to believe that a religious war today could transform this world into a paradise, whatever it might be, for God's faithful.

The *Ney* in the Mevlevi Tradition

Ney means 'reed' in Persian. It is the name given to all types of flutes made from this material. The one referred to in this book is the *ney* most commonly used and valued in the Arab, Persian and Turkish world, each using it in a style of its own. The origin of this instrument is lost in time immemorial. In some Egyptian tombs of the Pharaonic epoch there are depictions of flutes being played exactly in the same way as they are today. The simplicity of this instrument is a measure of its antiquity; the idea of shaping a reed to make a flute out of it is obvious. In spite of being so basic, it could be adapted to the traditional music of different countries. In Turkey, it occupies a special place and has acquired a deep meaning from the teachings of Mevlâna Celâleddin Rumi, the great Sufi master of the whirling dervishes from the thirteenth century.

One day, Rumi's disciple Husameddin Çelebi asked his master whether he intended to put his teaching in a written form. Rumi took out of his turban a roll of paper containing the first eighteen distichs (strophic units of two lines)of the *Mesnevî*, which he had just written. He asked his disciple to make a note of the commentary, which he improvised as he went along. This is how Çelebi wrote a further 24,000 verses starting from the first eighteen. They have become the essential basis of Rumi's teaching. Whoever starts on the *tariqa* (way) must first of all study the teaching.

Listen to the ney *telling a story,*
it laments its separation.

Thus begins the first distich of this poem. The *ney* here is a metaphor for a human being. Like a person, it is capable of expressing the tearing pain of separation. The reed, before becoming a flute, is separated from its watery environment: cut with a red-hot iron, emptied and cleaned out. Then it is pierced with seven holes. Humans have similar feelings of separation from their divine origins, even if they do not remember them. They are doomed to forget, to be distracted from the moment they are covered with flesh and subjected to their own natures. Just like the *ney*, people, inwardly purified, is freed from the obligations of the human condition. Like the *ney*, becoming available to the breath of the player, they can transmit the divine breath without sullying it.

Humans can be compared to the *ney*, which complains of being separated from its original environment. They are separated from the meeting of the spirits (*bezmi elest*, 'the meeting of eternity') , but keep it in unconscious memory and yearn for it. People suffer from the remoteness caused by the human condition. The *ney* evokes this state of separation. Its mournful-sounding melody resembles the words of a man who is directly inspired by God. Whoever hears this divine breath is brought to a state of remembrance, of recall of the Pure Spirit.

This is why when the *ney* was played in the Mevlevi brotherhoods, it was listened to as attentively as to the Qur'an or to the words of a 'conscious man'. Its profound meaning demands a compelling consideration. The *ney* has acquired a deep meaning from this first distich of the *Mesnevî*. In the Qur'an, the first word of revelation from God to the Prophet Muhammad is *ikra* ('tell'): 'Tell in the name of God' (*Ikra bi-ismi rabbuke*). Rumi begins his writings with the word *bishnev* ('listen' – i.e., 'listen to what has been revealed'). It is an invitation to listen to the revealed word in a more concrete way (as in the Qur'an) but also in a more abstract way – an invitation to listen to the music of the *ney* or the word of one called a 'Sufi'.

> *Since I have been cut from the reed bed*
> *my sorrow makes man and woman weep.*

The reed bed is the 'country of origin' of the reed. It grows amongst its peers. For humans, this original state is the pure spirit state before being clothed in flesh. The reed says, 'my sorrow makes man [*merd*] and woman [*zenne*] weep.' The words 'man' and 'woman' must not be taken here in the ordinary gender connotation. They mean two stages of evolution: one, when human beings are enslaved ('woman'), another when they are liberated ('man') from their own natures. Therefore, there can be men who are 'women', or *vice versa.*

I need a heart torn by separation to pour into it the pain of desire.

What is meant here is the wish or feeling to find again the state which has been lost by humans in their descent to earth. We must remember that the word *ney* represents human beings, who need to share their sorrow, caused by the separation, with others who have reached the same state of consciousness. They feel the need to be in *sympathy* with others who are in the same painful state of consciousness. Thus, the human-*ney* feels the need to tell and share his or her experience. It is this same need which led Rumi to write his work on the *ney.*

These concepts of separation and of union are basic in Sufi teachings. I remember that one day, when going to visit Rumi's mother's tomb near Konya, I visited the *tekke* that surrounded it (it no longer exists today; it has been replaced by a simple place for prayer). There I met, by chance, some members of the Arusiya brotherhood whose *sheik*, Aziz Çinar, used to go to the Uzbek *tekke* in Istanbul. Delighted to see me, they asked me to play the *ney* for the ceremony of *zikr* which was then taking place. While I was playing, the *sheik* came close to me and murmured in my ear, 'This is no lament caused by the separation; the song of the *ney* is the cry of joy of the union.'

Seen from this point of view, the *ney*, when played, is united to the breath of the player; likewise, one cannot speak of separation for the human being inspired by the divine breath. Maybe the moments of separation for the *ney* are those when it is not played, when it is not united with the lips of the player, and for human beings, those when the divine breath does not pass through them. Therefore, the *ney* is always anxious to meet whoever shares the same sorrow. It is the same for humans, since in nature each one looks for his equal.

Whoever remains far from his source
aspires to the moment when he will be united with it again.

People who are far from their original state seek the breath, the wind which will bring them back to these origins. The word 'origin' can be understood in all its aspects; it can just as well mean the idea of 'Fatherland' as that *of bezmi elest*, the return to eternity in a state of pure spirit. Anyone who becomes aware again of the original state of purity or freedom seeks the breath which can bring them back to it.

> *I enjoyed all gatherings*
> *I joined in with those who rejoice*
> *as well as with those who cry.*

Literally, these lines are not to do with 'crying' or 'rejoicing'. The words *bed halan* mean those who are in a bad state of mind, and the words *hos halan*, those who are in a pleasant state of mind. In other words: 'I went to all gatherings (*cemaat*), I mixed with those who cried just as well as with those who rejoiced.' Rumi, the *ney*, or awakened human beings make no distinction between the groups they frequent.

In this connection, I recall a passage from Rumi's life. Around him, there were people on the fringe of society, thieves and tramps. Those who did not like Rumi said about him, 'If Rumi was a respectable man, he would not deal with such people.' When he heard these critical remarks he replied, 'If they were in a better state of mind, I would be the one who would go to them. It is right that they should come to me.' Here we find the idea, as Hafez of Shiraz would say, of the 'need for blasphemy'. For if there was no blasphemy there would be no fire of Hell – as Saadi would say, 'I am in love with the whole universe because it is God's work.' Those who are in a bad state are equally part of the divine design.

For the conscious human being, as well as for the *ney*, there must be no distinction between those who are worthy and those who are not. In the Sufi way, there is no dichotomy between the good and bad people. The latter are in a constant state of evolution; whoever is bad today can be good tomorrow, and *vice versa*. In many anecdotes, Rumi tries to make us understand that the most pious and righteous people can, any day, commit the most horrible crimes. What matters to a Sufi is the becoming of a human; what they are today, be it good or bad, is of no importance. The transient aspect must not count. This is why many Sufis and awakened people found themselves in close proximity to others in whatever state they might have been.

> *Each one understood me according to his own feelings*
> *But none sought to know my secrets.*

The *ney* does not discriminate, but comes quite naturally according to whoever hears it. Whatever happens, each person feels he or she has shared something with the *ney*, with the awakened human being. Few amongst them, however, try to seek and understand the secret through which they have been touched, be it from the words of the enlightened person or the sound of the *ney*. This is an important point: many people listen to the *ney* simply as a musical instrument. Touched by the beauty of the sound or the melody, they just take the *ney* as the instrument of pure music; their pleasure is limited to the sensory realm. For many, the *Mesnevî* is only beautiful poetry. However, for a wise person, an awakened person, the sound of the *ney* reveals the secret that others have not heard.

Today there is much emphasis on 'religious' music, on 'Sufi' music, but one must understand these only as labels attached to the music. The religious or Sufi dimension depends only on the one who listens to it. The music itself is devoid of any intention of this kind. The *ney* in many Muslim countries is only a musical instrument, but for some people, such as the Sufis, apart from the cultural aspect it can represent a language, a discourse which carries a secret that it tries to transmit. The same is true for people. Traditionally, such or such a person can be seen as a Sufi, as being a 'master', but this is only a word corresponding to a specific cultural area. If one is to be touched, it must not be by the outer appearance of these people, or by the sound of the *ney* which also represents only the outer manifestation of this instrument; one must be touched by the secret that is hidden beyond the sensory perception. In the following distich, Rumi explains what the secret is that has been forgotten:

My secret however is not far from my sorrow
But neither ear nor eye know how to perceive it.

The eye and the ear do not have the *nûr* (light) to perceive the secret. It is not to do with knowing how to perceive, but rather being able to; the ear and the eye do not have the 'light' which allows the secret to be captured. Our senses depend on something else. The sense of sight, for instance, needs light to function. Here, we are concerned with a vision beyond what is ordinarily seen, a hearing beyond what is normally heard. There is an anecdote from Rumi's life which illustrates this:

One day, a theologian went to see Rumi and said, 'You, who are a good man, how is it that you invented this heresy of listening to music? What does it mean for you?' Rumi answered, 'When I listen to music, I hear the creaking of the opening of the gates of Heaven.' The theologian retorted, 'And yet, when I listen to music I hear no such thing.'

Rumi then smiled and said, 'Of course you hear it, but what you perceive is the creaking of the gates as they close.'

There exists a perception other than that which is given through music, poetry or speech. This perception, which Rumi calls the 'secret', depends on another 'light' that enables our senses to share the sorrow of the *ney*, unveiling its secret.

*The body is not hidden to the soul, nor the soul to the body
However, no one can see the soul.*

The secret of the body is the soul. But is it really a secret? If one perceives the body, one knows it is inhabited by the soul; if one hears the *ney*, one knows that the breath of the musician passes through it. But it is not given to all to perceive the soul. As it is said in the Qur'an: 'Tell them that the soul is under divine order and that men will know very little about it.' The secret in the *ney*, the secret which is in the awakened one, is as evident as the spirit in the body, but few can perceive this.

The sound of the ney *is fire, not wind.
He who lacks this flame will come to nothing.*

The word 'wind' here must be understood as air, which has a double meaning in this context. It is first of all the source of bodily influences, ambitions or desires. In other words, the sound of the *ney* does not come from any bodily desire, and the words of an awakened person do not come from his or her own desires or ambitions, but from the fire of love. Rumi goes on to say, 'Whoever does not have this fire, let him come to nothing.' This nothingness can wrongly be understood as a curse. Quite the opposite, it is a prayer for those who have no flames to be burned by the fire of love (many Sufi masters say that divine treasures reside in inexistence and nothingness). Rumi wishes that those who do not perceive the sound of the *ney* as the fire of love, but only as a pleasure given by the senses, come to nothingness. Only the annihilation of their passion and their misunderstanding will allow them to be touched by this flame of love, which rises from the *ney* or from the words of a wise individual.

*It is the fire of love which is in the reed
It is the heat of love which makes the wine bubble.*

The fire in the *ney* and the bubbling of the wine are the work of love. The love spoken of here is beyond all passion. In the Qur'an , the word used for 'love' is *mohabett* (the one who has love within him). In the second *sura*, verse 165, it is written that the faithful have 'very strong' *mohabett*: a very strong passion for God. The same word can be found in verse 30 of Joseph's *sura*, where it speaks of Zuleka's love for Joseph: '*mohabett* surrounded his heart like a thin film.' It means that the word implies subjugation, to no longer see anyone else but the beloved.

This extreme passion for a human being can also be physical. In Sufi teachings this passion is understood as 'suggested love' (*ashq-i-medjaz*) or as love of Truth, 'real love' (*ashq-i-khaqiqat*). One can lead to the other. In Middle Eastern Islamic literature there are frequent descriptions of great passion for a human being which is transmuted into 'real love'. The story of Majnun and Leila is an example. Majnun is so much in love with his beloved that he can no longer recognise her; he sees something of Leila in all creatures; it is a total burst of passion.

Sufism teaches that love is not an impulse of a person towards the beloved, but rather an attraction, an aspiration which comes from the Beloved. The roles are reversed: the human being is not active, it is the Creator who attracts the human being towards Him. Carnal love or any other ordinary passion is only a trap in its exclusivity.

When Abraham destroyed the idols of the temple, he spared one and attached the axe he had just been using around its neck. Horrified, the worshippers asked who could have committed such a sacrilegious crime. Abraham then told them that the idol which was untouched and had the axe around its neck was responsible. The worshippers replied that this was impossible, for how could a statue act in such a way? Abraham answered, 'If it is only a statue, how can it be a divinity?'

A single passion, as in the case of the idols, destroys all others, and cleanses the human heart of the ridicule of the attachment to passion – the heart is considered a temple. Love comes from divine inspiration. The fire of love which arises from the *ney* is of divine inspiration, just like the bubbling of the wine. The drunkenness caused by wine is a theological prohibition in Islam, as it is an obstacle to prayer. In the Qur'an, it is said, 'Do not approach prayer in a state of intoxication.' There are a number of rules concerning the fruit of the vine. For example, it is not permitted to eat grapes before they are ripe and sweet. It is permitted to drink grape juice, but not when it is fermented. It is not permitted to drink wine, but the use of vinegar is allowed. Wine, seen by the Sufi, is the poetic symbol of the inspired word, as the latter causes a state of intoxication which is comparable to that caused by wine. Therefore here, what is meant by 'love' is a transformation of good or bad states, permissible or not, that any creature can undergo. Love, the great divine inspiration, makes anyone who is inspired live through various states.

> *The* ney *is the confidant of one who is separated from his Friend*
> *His accents tear the veil.*

The *ney* or enlightened person is one who feels the separation from the 'Friend'. This refers to the idea of reunion mentioned earlier, *bezmi elest*, the gathering in eternity where all spirits heard, 'Do you recognise that I am your Lord? ' (The spirits answered in the affirmative.) The *ney*, considered the confidant, is the one who remembers this moment. It represents a state of awakening in relation to everything that distracts us in this world.

The melodies arising from the *ney* tear the veils which prevent us from reaching the Truth. The word *perde* (veil) is often found in Sufism. Non-understanding, sleepiness or distraction are states called *perde*. In its musical sense, each sound is also called *perde*. There is, therefore, a similarity of meaning for this word; it is at the same time the veil, and also a degree in the musical scale. In fact, each hole pierced in the *ney* is also called *perde*. Each one represents an opening of our senses, like as many veils being torn. What is captured by our senses remains veiled. The wine of the sage or the sound of the *ney* tears open the veil of what appears to our senses.

> *Who ever saw a poison and an antidote like the* ney?
> *Who ever saw a comforter and a lover like the* ney?

The *ney* (or the sage): poison and antidote.

Understanding or super-consciousness is not always easy to conceive. Remaining with the idea of love, the fact of being conscious of this separation, the fact that the sound of the *ney* or the words of the sage make us remember, make us become aware again of this separation, poisons our lives. The state of forgetfulness, of distraction, is in a certain way pleasant for us, even if it is to the detriment of the values which preside at the banquet of Truth. In this way, the *ney* is a poison. It is also an antidote because it comforts those who are conscious of this separation. The *ney* is what makes one fall in love, but also what comforts one from the pain of love.

Fariduddin Attâr, the great Sufi whom Rumi speaks of in his writings with the utmost respect, makes use of a metaphor to illustrate this idea:

A man, falling into a well, just manages to hang on to a dead branch of a tree growing around it. The branch nearly splits. A fatal fall is imminent. He then notices, with fright, that a dragon at the bottom of the well is trying to get hold of his legs. Mastering his fear, he sees, close to him, a beehive full of honey. While holding on with one hand, he takes a little honey with the other, tastes it and says, 'Life, what a joy!'

The *ney* acts as a reminder of the precarious, the ephemeral situation of our life. The taste of honey can make us forget danger, make us lose our awareness of it.

The ney *speaks of the bloodstained path of love*
and reminds us of the story of Majnun's passion.

The reed pulled out from the pond, cut, burned clean, then pierced with holes to allow the melody to rise, is the tearing, the bloodstained path of the *ney*. For man, any desire is a bloodstained path. There is a fundamental Sufi teaching which comes from the very words of the Prophet: *Mutu qable ente mutu* ('die before dying'); It relates to the death of all passions except the passion for the Beloved. This idea is made clear in the story of Majnun and Leila. Majnun is the hero of this passionate love story, but the name 'Majnun' itself can mean 'madness'. In other words, it is the story of a love which leads to madness.

In this distich, Rumi wants to convey that he who is not in love can see love as a bloodstained path.

This reminds me of the story of a man who suffered from eczema. He went to consult a doctor, who prescribed an ointment that, the man was told, would get rid of the problem before long. The man then asked, 'Doctor, can I continue to have the pleasure of scratching myself?'

The fact of no longer being able to 'scratch oneself' can appear as a bloodstained path.

The inspiration, or rather the aspiration brought about by the Creator, leads to the relinquishment of what is useless or futile. The abandonment of these things can seem painful to those who are not inspired. This is what happens in the story of Majnun and Leila; Majnun, who has fallen madly in love with Leila, goes off to the desert to live amongst wild beasts. His friends take pity on him because of the madness he is living through. But from his viewpoint, his situation is in no way deserving of pity.

It is possible to consider this distich from another level: such a love undoubtedly is endless for, as many Eastern poets have written, love exists only in a situation of separation. In the state of union, in as much as there is fusion with the beloved, love no longer exists. The sorrow, the lament, is engendered by the distance from the object of love; the awareness of this separation is 'poisoning', 'bloodstaining'. The more this awareness increases, the more the desire to be united with the Beloved (God) grows. This fusion is only conceivable after the 'dying before dying', that is to say, the dilution of the self in the divine will.

> *In the* Garden of Roses, *Saadi, the great Sufi poet, recounts that one day while he was in a garden, he saw a nightingale with a rose petal in its beak. The bird was crying for the rose. The poet then said, 'O Nightingale, why are you crying for the rose when you are in a garden full of them, and in your beak you even have a petal?' The nightingale retorted, 'O Poet, this is no concern of yours! This is just a caprice between the rose and myself!'*

Rumi writes:

> *Only he who has renounced his senses is entrusted with the meaning.*
> *The tongue has no other listener than the ear.*

Rumi shows here that, in order to reach a certain level of understanding, one has to get rid of discursive reasoning. In Persian, the word *hûsh* means 'intelligence', 'reasoning'. The word *bîhûsh* means 'madness'. Only those who are in a certain state of 'madness' can be close to this understanding. The intelligence of the heart is a light granted to people to understand Truth. The painful path of love, 'bloodstained' as Rumi calls it, can be seen as pure aberration by those who do not possess this intelligence. This is how Majnun, wandering in the desert and wild with love, is considered mad by those who are the bearers of ordinary reason. As for Majnun, he knows intimately how to approach Truth without the interference of any pondering.

> *In our affliction, days have become gloomy*
> *Our days travel with burning pain.*

As is common in Eastern poetry, Rumi speaks directly to his interlocutor in order to insist on a fact. He incites him not to waste time: days passed in unconsciousness are spent in burning pain.

If our days have fled by, no matter!
Stay, o you, comparable to none.

No matter if time passes by, comforts Rumi. The enlightened person or the *ney* remains. The awakened one is hope, and gives hope to those who have not yet reached this level of consciousness. Like the awakened one, like the *ney*, one day you, too, will be able to burn with the fire of Love; you, too, will be able to transmit divine inspiration.

Whoever is not a fish quenches his thirst with His water
Whoever is deprived of his daily bread finds the day long.

The literal translation of *mâhî* is 'what lives in the water'. *Bîruzî* ('he who is deprived') has a double meaning. It can refer to food for the body, but also that for the spirit. Those whose sustenance comes from the food for the body will later be granted the sustenance given by the food for the spirit. It is only a matter of time.

According to the *Mesnevî* commentaries, there are three kinds of people. There are those who have not yet been fully satisfied through prayer or invocation of God; just as the sand never seems to have enough water, they are never filled enough with food for the spirit. Others, who have only drunk a small cup, sink into drunkenness. They can take no more. Finally, there are those who have not yet tasted food for the spirit and do not even have the wish for it. The first two kinds of people are called *mâhî*, those who live in water. This is why Rumi writes, 'Apart from the fish, all others have been satisfied by water.' *Bîruzî* are those who do not yet know this divine state. To them days seem long because they do not have their daily bread. As they are impatient, Rumi comforts them by telling them that their sustenance will come later.

He who has no experience cannot understand the state of he who knows,
my words must therefore be brief. Adieu.

Rather than the lack of experience, it is more an absence of maturity that can be translated literally as the word *ham* ('raw'). Rumi underlines the fact that maturity can only be obtained through living, and not by discursive knowledge.

No understanding of these eighteen distichs on the *ney* is possible for those who are immature. Likewise, the *ney* only becomes mature and available to the breath of the player after its holes have been opened, and a person needs to reach a certain level of maturity to open to the words of the sage.

These eighteen distichs from Rumi's *Mesnevî* are a symbolic representation of the speech of the awakened person. In the many Sufi meetings I was fortunate to attend in my youth, I saw all these men listening to the *ney* with tears in their eyes. Traditionally, the place given to the *ney* in the whirling dervish ceremonies is foremost, even irreplaceable. The ceremony always begins with a long moment of meditation played on the *ney*, which introduces the proper music for the ceremony.

The Ceremony of
the Whirling Dervishes

All Sufi brotherhoods (*tariqa*) hold communal meetings called *zikr* (Turkish: 'invocation'). For most brotherhoods, these are weekly meetings. In these ceremonies a ritual is strictly followed in which the name of God is invoked to a specific rhythm of breathing together with the recitation of prayers and singing of hymns.

In the *tariqa* the *zikr* can either take place inwardly (*zikr hafi*, i.e. 'hidden') or can be expressed collectively (*zikr cehri*, i.e. 'evident'). In the whirling ceremony, this invocation is internal. Specific movements accompany the rhythms related to the invocations. In the movement known as *devran* (cycle), a ring is formed with precise steps and all the participants begin to turn to make a circle.

Amongst the whirling dervishes, the turning movements are individual and based on a very exact ritual. Their ceremonies differ from those of other Sufi brotherhoods. The brotherhood of the Mevlevi whirling dervishes owes its name to its founder, Mevlâna Celâleddin Rumi; the Mevlevi are the disciples of Mevlâna. The ceremony itself is called *sama'* (hearing). It involves listening to music specially composed for the ritual, and listening to the singing of Rumi's poems. Together they generate an inner 'shock' which expresses itself externally in a dance, a whirling movement.

On the day appointed for a *sama'*, the disciples gather in a vast room called *sama' hané* (the house of *sama'*). It has a wooden floor and, just as in a mosque, it contains a *mihrab* (prayer niche) and is therefore oriented towards Mecca.

After the recitation of the usual prayers, the master of the ceremony sits on a sheepskin post facing the *Kaaba*. (The sheepskin is the symbol of the *maqam*, or the representation of Rumi.) From the door of the *sama' hané* to the *mihrab* an imaginary line (*hatti ustuva*) is drawn which cuts the room in two. Its symbolic function is so respected that only the master may walk on it. The disciples sit to the left of the master in a place determined precisely by their positions in the hierarch. Seated opposite the master are the musicians, whose instruments are the same as those used in classical Turkish music . Amongst them, the *ney* (the reed flute) has a fundamental place.

The ceremony opens with a recitation from the Qur'an received in a meditative silence. Then the master begins the prayer, which is called *post duasi* (opening prayer) and consists of praise to the Prophet and the dedication of the ceremony to His companions, to Rumi and his successors as well as to all the faithful. The master proposes a *zikr* on the name 'Allah', lengthening the vowels. This is joined in by the disciples. Depending on the *tekke*, this invocation is repeated eleven, thirty-three or even ninety-nine times in a rhythm gradually accelerating from very slow to very fast. At the end of the count, the master says *Illallah* while continuing to lengthen the last vowel 'a'. Then follows a song called *naat*; its performance, particular to the brotherhood, has become a tradition since the second half of the seventeenth century. Mustafa Itri Dede, a musician of the brotherhood, composed this song from a poem by Rumi praising the Prophet.

The *naat* is followed by a *taksim* (improvisation) on the *ney* received in a state of inner calm. It must end in the musical mode corresponding to the composition to be interpreted afterwards. Around forty compositions have been created since the fourteenth century, and are specific to the ceremony of the whirling dervishes.

The composition starts with a prelude. After the introduction on the *ney*, the chief *ney* player, who at the same time is the leader of the musicians and the one who positioned next to the *sheik*, begins the prelude accompanied by the *kudum* in a rhythmic cycle of twenty-eight or fifty-six beats. The master and the disciples, who until then are seated, strike the floor with their hands and stand up.

All wear the *hirka* (a kind of long black coat) and the *sikke* (a tall felt hat) on their heads. The master, standing, bows his head to greet the disciples who in turn, bow to him. Then the *sheik* takes a few steps to his right and turns towards the disciple coming towards him. They both come forward on each side of the imaginary line, face each other, look straight at each other for a brief moment, and bow. The *sheik* then goes around the room of the *sama'*, walking very slowly, following the rhythm of the prelude. All the participants, in turn, make the same gestures as those which have been made by the master and his assistant, forming a kind of procession (Arabic: *moukabele*). These bows recall those which God asked the angels to make to Adam, whom He had just created (amongst all the angels, Satan was the only one to refuse). It represents the mark of respect given to the divine part in man. It is the most beautiful stage in the ceremony; the participants facing each other in complete silence, looking at each other and bowing.

The *sheik*, having walked three times round the room, then goes back to the sheepskin which is symbolically considered as the privileged place of the master.

The sung part of the composition then begins. The disciples take off their black coats and appear in long white robes. Each one in his turn walks towards the master and bows. The master kisses the headdress before him. Then, one after the other, they begin to whirl, the right foot pivoting around the left foot which remains fixed on the floor. The two arms are crossed on the chest in a gesture called *niyaz* (requesting). The disciple then raises his arms slowly to the level of his headdress and gradually opens them up completely. The palm of his right hand turned upwards towards the sky, while the left one is turned down towards the earth. The fingers are joined, except for the thumb. The head is slightly bent to the right and down towards his heart. While raising his right foot and pivoting on his left leg, he silently pronounces the syllable *Al*. At the end of the turn, when putting his right foot on the ground, he silently pronounces the syllable *Lah*. So he whirls, following the given rhythmic cycle while pronouncing the name of *Allah*.

The compositions used for the event are masterpieces of Sufi music and classical Turkish music. The bowing is repeated four times. At the end of the first, the rhythm changes. In general, the cycle of fourteen beats becomes a slow cycle of 9/4 or 9/2 called *evfer*. Then the disciples all stand still and bow to the master. Each dancer, with his eyes closed, lets the big toe of his right foot rest on his left foot. Then he rejoins the other disciples. When they come together again, each one touches the shoulder of his neighbour, and again they take their positions to the left of the master, while taking care not to step on the imaginary line. The second round of bowing then begins. At the fourth bowing the *sheik* himself takes an active part in the *sama'*. Keeping his black coat on, he places himself on the imaginary line and, whirling very slowly, moves towards the centre of the room and stays there for a moment. He then returns to his sheepskin. This is the end of the dance. The ceremony closes with the recitation from the Qur'an. The disciples stand still, and while reciting prayers, they put on their long black coats. Then, after a last bow to the master, they all leave the room. During the ceremony, no word is said and no gesture is made other than those required by the ritual.

The ceremony is like a flower which opens slowly after the meditative recitation of the Qur'an. While the dance manifests deep ecstasy, no liberties are allowed as to its expression. The disciples show the deepest respect towards each other; each one contains his emotions and restrains the cries of joy which might occur during his ecstasy. Although the ritual is full of movement, it is nonetheless lived inwardly.

Nowadays, these ceremonies are rarely practised. Some brotherhoods in Turkey or in the Arab world (like the whirling dervishes of Damascus and Aleppo) perform the whirling dance without the ceremonial music or the ritual. To be performed in its entirety, the ceremony demands a deep knowledge of the ritual gestures.

Music from the *Tekke* of Istanbul
from the archives of Kudsi Erguner

1. Composition: *Taksim* (in the *maqam Rast*)   (5'56")
   Artist: Suleyman Erguner Dede (*ney*)
   Recorded in 1952 by Hulusi Gokmenli at the Uzbek *tekke*.
   The melodic development of this improvisation only uses the range of a fifth; despite the limited use of intervals, it is astonishing to note the great inventiveness of the melody.

2. Composition: *Allah Diyelim*, (*ilahi* in the *maqam Rast*)   (2'30")
   Recorded in 1980 by Kudsi Erguner at the Fatih Mosque in Istanbul during a memorial ceremony for Ulvi Erguner.

3. Composition: *Taksim* (in the *maqam Saba*)   (3'15")
   Artist: Ulvi Erguner (*ney*)

4. Composition: *Halati Vasl* (*ghazal* in the *maqam Saba*)   (3'52")
   Artist: Cevdet Soydanses
   Recorded in 1969 by Pierre-Marie Goulet during a *sam'a* at the Uzbek *tekke*.

5. Composition: *Taksim* (in the *maqam Ussak*)   (3'55")
   Artist: Ulvi Erguner (*ney*)

6. Composition (by Suleyman Erguner Dede): *Noldu bu Gönlüm* (*ilahi* in the *maqam Ussak*)   (2'05")
   Recorded in 1980 by Kudsi Erguner at the Fatih Mosque in Istanbul during a memorial ceremony for Ulvi Erguner.

7. Composition: *Taksim* (in the *maqam Hicaz*)   (3'30")
Artist: Ulvi Erguner (*ney*)

8. Composition: *Gönül Mazhardir* (*ilahi* in the *maqam Beyatiaraban*)   (1'20")
Recorded in 1980 by Kudsi Erguner at the Fatih Mosque in Istanbul during a memorial ceremony for Ulvi Erguner.

9. Composition (by Yusuf Bilgin): *Ey Kasifi Huda Mevlâna* (*ghazal* in the *maqam Ussak*)   (4'50")
Artist: Yusuf Bilgin (vocals)
Recorded in 1981 at *Ayini Cem*, a Mevlevi ceremony; the song is a poem in praise of Rumi.

10. Composition: *Taksim* (in the *maqam Segah*)   (2'20")
Artist: Suleyman Erguner Dede (*ney*)

11. Composition (by Tamburi Cemil Bey): *Peshrev* (in the *maqam Seddiaraban*)   (5'10")
Artists: Ulvi Erguner, Niyazi Sayin, Aka Gündüz Kutbay and Dogan Ergin (*ney* ensemble) Recorded in 1970.

12. Composition: *Taksim* (in the *maqam Segah*)   (3'50")
Artist: Ulvi Erguner (*ney*)

13. Composition: *Gül Yüzünü* (*ilahi* in the *maqam Huzzam*)   (2'05")

14. Composition: *Taksim* (in the *maqam Nihavend*)   (4'10")
Artist: Suleyman Erguner Dede (*ney*)

15. Composition: *Yüzünü Dergaha Tut* (*ghazal* in the *maqam Rast*)   (6'45")
Artist: Huseyn Sebilci (vocals)
Recorded in 1967 by Pierre-Marie Goulet at the Cerrahiya *tekke* under the direction of Sheik Muzaffer Ozak.

16. Composition: *Taksim* (in the *maqam Acemasiran*)   (3'40")
Artist: Kudsi Erguner (*ney*)

17. Composition: *Uyan ey Gozlerim* (*ghazal* in the *maqam Muhayyer*)   (5'30")
Artist: Yusuf Bilgin (vocals)
Recorded in 1980 by Kudsi Erguner at the Fatih Mosque in Istanbul during a memorial ceremony for Ulvi Erguner.